JIM BOWIE

Other titles in *Historical American Biographies*

Alexander Graham Bell
Inventor and Teacher
ISBN 0-7660-1096-1

Andrew Carnegie
Steel King and
Friend to Libraries
ISBN 0-7660-1212-3

Annie Oakley
Legendary Sharpshooter
ISBN 0-7660-1012-0

Benjamin Franklin
Founding Father and
Inventor
ISBN 0-89490-784-0

Billy the Kid
Outlaw of the Wild West
ISBN 0-7660-1091-0

Buffalo Bill Cody
Western Legend
ISBN 0-7660-1015-5

Clara Barton
Civil War Nurse
ISBN 0-89490-778-6

Daniel Boone
Frontier Legend
ISBN 0-7660-1256-5

Dolley Madison
Courageous First Lady
ISBN 0-7660-1092-9

George Armstrong Custer
Civil War General and
Western Legend
ISBN 0-7660-1255-7

Jane Addams
Nobel Prize Winner and
Founder of Hull House
ISBN 0-7660-1094-5

Jeb Stuart
Confederate Cavalry General
ISBN 0-7660-1013-9

Jefferson Davis
President of the Confederacy
ISBN 0-7660-1064-3

Jesse James
Legendary Outlaw
ISBN 0-7660-1055-4

Jim Bowie
Hero of the Alamo
ISBN 0-7660-1253-0

John Wesley Powell
Explorer of the
Grand Canyon
ISBN 0-89490-783-2

Lewis and Clark
Explorers of the Northwest
ISBN 0-7660-1016-3

Louisa May Alcott
Author of Little Women
ISBN 0-7660-1254-9

Mark Twain
Legendary Writer
and Humorist
ISBN 0-7660-1093-7

Martha Washington
First Lady
ISBN 0-7660-1017-1

Mary Todd Lincoln
Tragic First Lady
of the Civil War
ISBN 0-7660-1252-2

Paul Revere
Rider for the
Revolution
ISBN 0-89490-779-4

Robert E. Lee
Southern Hero of the
Civil War
ISBN 0-89490-782-4

Robert Fulton
Inventor and
Steamboat Builder
ISBN 0-7660-1141-0

Stonewall Jackson
Confederate General
ISBN 0-89490-781-6

Susan B. Anthony
Voice for Women's
Voting Rights
ISBN 0-89490-780-8

Thomas Alva Edison
Inventor
ISBN 0-7660-1014-7

Thomas Nast
Political Cartoonist
ISBN 0-7660-1251-4

The Wright Brothers
Inventors of
the Airplane
ISBN 0-7660-1095-3

Historical American Biographies

JIM BOWIE

Hero of the Alamo

Ann Graham Gaines

Enslow Publishers, Inc.

40 Industrial Road	PO Box 38
Box 398	Aldershot
Berkeley Heights, NJ 07922	Hants GU12 6BP
USA	UK

http://www.enslow.com

Library of Congress Cataloging-in-Publication Data

Gaines, Ann.
    Jim Bowie : hero of the Alamo / Ann Graham Gaines.
       p. cm. — (Historical American biographies)
    Includes bibliographical references and indexes.
    Summary: Traces the life of the frontier settler and Texas defender
who died in the attack on the Alamo, including information on his early
days and his effect on American frontier culture.
    ISBN 0-7660-1253-0
    1. Bowie, James, d. 1836 Juvenile literature. 2. Pioneers—Texas
Biography Juvenile literature. 3. Alamo (San Antonio, Tex.)—Siege, 1836
Juvenile literature. 4. Texas—History—To 1846 Juvenile literature.
[1. Bowie, James, d. 1836. 2. Pioneers. 3. Alamo (San Antonio, Tex.)—
Siege, 1836. 4. Texas—History—Revolution, 1835–1836.] I. Title.
II. Series.
F389.B8G35   2000
976.4'03'092
[B]—DC21   99-14239
                                             CIP

Printed in the United States of America

10 9 8 7 6 5 4 3 2 1

To Our Readers:
All Internet addresses in this book were active and appropriate when we
went to press. Any comments or suggestions can be sent by e-mail to
Comments@enslow.com or to the address on the back cover.

Illustration Credits: Enslow Publishers, Inc., pp. 16, 54, 89, 102, 108;
*Ready-to-Use Authentic Civil War Illustrations: 245 Copyright-Free
Designs Printed One Side*, Published by Dover Publications, 1995, p. 25;
Reproduced from the *Dictionary of American Portraits*, Published by
Dover Publications, Inc., in 1967, pp. 20, 22, 29, 65, 91, 93; Texas
Department of Transportation, pp. 8, 11, 31, 37, 46, 71, 72, 78, 110, 111.

Cover Illustration: Reproduced from the *Dictionary of American
Portraits*, Published by Dover Publications, Inc., in 1967 (Inset); Texas
Department of Transportation (Background—The Alamo).

CONTENTS

1

THE ALAMO

An old church, the Alamo, in San Antonio, Texas, is maintained today as a shrine. It was the scene of a battle during the war for Texas independence from Mexico in 1836 in which all of the Texan defenders were killed by the forces of Mexican General Antonio López de Santa Anna. Some of the men who died there are well known: Jim Bowie, Davy Crockett, and William Barret Travis. All the Texans who died there, famous or not, knew that they would die if they defended the Alamo, but determined that it was worth the sacrifice.

The Battle of the Alamo

As the Mexican troops approached San Antonio from the south, the Texans fell back behind the

The Alamo served as the site of the most dramatic battle in the fight for the independence of Texas from Mexico.

fortified walls around the Alamo. The Mexicans surrounded the Alamo and called for its surrender. The Texans refused. The Mexicans attacked before dawn on March 6, 1836.

The Mexican attack was made by companies of men who attacked a few vulnerable points in the walls of the mission. Valiant officers led their men up ladders and over the walls. The Texans shot them at point-blank range, killing a man with almost every bullet they fired. Cannons loaded with nails and chain links killed twenty to thirty men at once. Hundreds of Mexican soldiers were killed almost immediately.

The Mexican officers who survived the first assault continued the attack. The Texans fought in small pockets from wherever they could find cover. Finally, the Mexican troops reached the Texans and were victorious in the hand-to-hand knife and bayonet clashes that finally ended the Texans' lives.

It was all over by six in the morning. When General Santa Anna arrived on the scene,

> he could see for himself the . . . devastated area littered with corpses, with scattered limbs and bullets, with weapons and torn uniforms. Some of these were burning together with the corpses, which produced an unbearable and nauseating odor. The bodies, with their blackened and bloody faces disfigured by a desperate death, their hair and uniforms burning at once, presented a dreadful and truly hellish sight.[1]

The Alamo
In 1719, alarmed by the lack of local defense, the Spanish government in Mexico established missions in the middle of Texas. By 1793, however, the government had closed all its Texas missions as unnecessary. The religious functions of the San Antonio Mission were given to the church, and the lands of the mission were given to the citizens of San Antonio. The mission structures were used as a barracks for a cavalry unit from the town of San José y Santiago del Alamo de Parras. Soon everyone was calling the mission the "Alamo." By the 1820s, the cavalry unit from Parras was gone. The Alamo Mission was mainly deserted except for a few poor families who found shelter in its decaying structure.[2]

The Texan Dead

Santa Anna ordered town officials to identify the Texan leaders. William Barret Travis, shot once in the forehead, was found on the north side of the compound.[3] Davy Crockett was found at the door to the Alamo chapel, surrounded by dead Mexican soldiers.[4] Jim Bowie was found on his hospital bed in a small room in the southwest corner of the Alamo chapel.[5] Santa Anna ordered town officials to burn the bodies of the Texan defenders.

The Mexican cavalry captured citizens of the town and forced them to make two large funeral

The Alamo, though heavily fortified, failed to protect the Texas defenders from the heavy attack of Santa Anna's Mexican forces.

pyres. When they had created large stacks of bodies and wood, they poured oil and grease all over them. At five in the afternoon, they lit the bonfires.[6]

The Mexican Dead

Santa Anna then ordered that the Mexican dead be buried. He did not realize that there were simply too many bodies. Four officers were buried with a religious ceremony in San Fernando Church. Several other officers and a few enlisted men were buried in the local cemetery. That was all the room there was. There was not enough firewood or cooking oil to cremate them. Many were included with the Texan defenders on their funeral pyres.[7] Nearly half of the eight hundred Mexican dead were thrown into the San Antonio River.

Who Were the Alamo Defenders?

The Alamo defenders sold their lives dearly. At least eight Mexican soldiers died for each one of the Texans. What kind of men were these Alamo defenders? Why were they capable of such savage courage, daring, and will? This is the story of the life of one of the Alamo defenders, Jim Bowie.

2

EARLY LIFE

At the age of thirteen, Jim Bowie's father, Rezin Bowie, fought in the American Revolution. It was a time of exciting adventure for a teenager:

> At the storming of Savannah he was wounded and taken prisoner. In warding off a blow directed at his head by a British officer, his hand was nearly severed by the saber of the English-man. While confined in Savannah his wounds were dressed by the patriotic women of that city, among whom was Elve Ap-Catesby Jones, daughter of John Jones, a Welsh emigrant. Young Bowie lost his heart [to] . . . his nurse, and married her in 1782, when not twenty years of age.[1]

Elve, Jim's mother, was a woman of rugged character—respectful, pious, and endowed with as much courage as any man. Raised on the rough frontier, she was a fit partner for her sturdy spouse when they set up their home near the Savannah River in Burke County, Georgia, after the war ended.[2]

Together, the young couple had ten children. Their first children were twin girls, Lavinia and Lavisia, who were born in 1783. Both girls died when they were babies. Their oldest son, David, was born in 1784. He was a sickly child and died in his teens. John was born in 1785, followed by Sarah in 1787. By then, Rezin was unhappy with life in Burke County, which is located along the Georgia-South Carolina border. The family packed the possessions they could carry in a wagon and began a series of moves into the unexplored forests on the western frontier of the newly created United States.

Life on the Frontier

The Bowies were among the first settlers on the frontier. They shared the land with the American Indians. Whenever they moved, they would erect a cabin alongside a clear running stream, close to where they could fish and hunt. After a few years, the deer, turkey, and fish would not be as plentiful. Then, the Bowies, like many other pioneer families, would move on, away from any newly arrived neighbors. Neighbors often presented problems that ranged from crime to disease. It was often easier simply to move as the closely knit Bowie family continued to grow. The Bowies moved to Elliott

Springs, Tennessee, about 1789, when daughter Mary was born. Martha was born in 1791, and Rezin Pleasant was born on September 8, 1793.

The lands of the frontier at that time were free to the pioneers who claimed them first. There was always a profit to be made, selling these freely acquired lands to new settlers. Getting land for nothing and selling it for money was one of Rezin Bowie's favorite pastimes. On November 10, 1793, he claimed 640 acres on Station Camp Creek, a mile west of Gallatin, Tennessee. Just two months later, he sold almost half of it. There is no record of what happened to the other half. It is very possible that the Bowies either gave it away or simply deserted it when they moved to Kentucky in 1794.[3]

The family moved to Logan County, Kentucky, bringing along three slaves and five horses. There, James, known as Jim, was born on April 10, 1796.[4] By 1797, the Bowies owned two hundred acres alongside the Read River, as well as nine slaves and eleven horses.[5] The Bowies lived well, raising and selling cattle.

Frontier Family Life

The frontier was free, but it was not an environment for the fainthearted. Frontier families were tightly knit, and family members protected one another. Young children on the frontier grew up in a hurry. They acted and were treated as men and women by the age of thirteen or fourteen, sometimes even younger. From earliest childhood, the children were needed and expected to contribute to the survival of the family. Usually, there were no schools in the wilderness for children to attend. None of the Bowie children ever went to school, yet all of them learned to read, write, and do arithmetic from lessons taught by Elve. Jim Bowie became fluent in speaking and writing Spanish, French, and English. His surviving letters are clear and well spelled. It is remarkable that Elve found time among the many jobs of each and every day to truly educate all of her children.

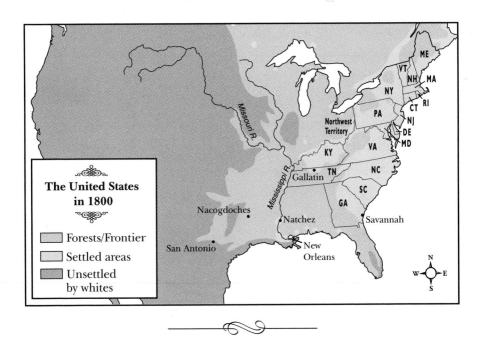

The Bowie family moved to the western frontier of the United States in the late 1700s, which at the time reached only as far as the present-day states of Kentucky, Tennessee, and Missouri.

In 1800, the Bowies sold their land in Kentucky, crossed the Mississippi River, and left the United States for the Spanish province of Upper Louisiana, which today is Missouri. In those days, there were few formal borders between states and countries. People traveled through the forests and down the rivers wherever they wanted. The Bowies moved down the Mississippi River to present-day Louisiana in 1802. They settled on the Bushley Bayou in what later became Catahoula Parish. In 1809 they moved to nearby Bayou Teche, and in 1812 to Opelousas Parish.[6]

Growing Up in Louisiana

Jim Bowie was six years old when his family moved to Louisiana, where he grew into manhood. Besides their school lessons, Jim Bowie and his brothers and sisters quickly learned the survival skills of the wilderness. They learned to use a rifle, pistol, snares, and traps. They took care of the family horses, pigs, and cattle. They worked in the garden, planted corn, and could speak several American Indian dialects. From the Indians, they learned about medicines, nature lore, and how to use a bow and arrow and a knife.

Frontier work was hard, and there was plenty to do every day, but there was always time for fun as well. Most days included time for hunting, fishing, and the youthful adventures of roping the wild horses and cattle that roamed on the remote islands of the bayou swamps. For even more excitement, young men would sometimes wrestle the alligators that were also plentiful in the rivers and swamps. Jim was reputed to be a champion alligator wrestler.

Jim Bowie grew strong in this natural school of life. He and his brothers would cut trees, saw them into boards, raft the boards to New Orleans, and sell them for spending money.

Marching Off to War

After the end of the American Revolution, there continued to be conflict between the new United States and Great Britain. The War of 1812 was fought to get the British out of American territory for good and to firmly establish American independence. By 1814, the British were set to invade the United States. However, a defeat of the British fleet at Lake Champlain helped convince Great Britain to sign a treaty ending the war on December 24, 1814.

Before the treaty was signed, a call went out in December 1814 for volunteers to fight the expected British invasion of New Orleans. Jim Bowie and his older brother Rezin joined the 17th Regiment from Rapides Parish as privates. Jim was eighteen and Rezin twenty-one years old.

Certainly the thrill of marching off to war, just as their father had done nearly forty years before, must have filled the brothers' hearts as they went to enlist. The regiment marched for New Orleans on January 8, 1815, the same day that American

General Andrew Jackson defeated the British at the Battle of New Orleans, decisively ending the war. The Bowie brothers were not needed after all. The volunteer regiments remained in New Orleans until the middle of March, when they were disbanded and the men were sent home.[7]

Striking Out on His Own

Around this time, Jim Bowie moved away from his family home. He cleared a small area from the forest and built a cabin at Bayou Boeuf in Rapides Parish.[8] He then began to enlarge his circle of acquaintances in the social worlds that centered on the cities of New Orleans and nearby Natchez. His brother John remembered him then:

> After reaching the age of maturity he was a stout, rather raw-boned man, of six feet height, weighed 180 pounds, and about as well made as any man I ever saw. His hair was light-colored, not quite red—his eyes were gray, rather deep set in his head, very keen and penetrating in their glance; his complexion fair, and his cheek-bones rather high. Taken altogether, he was a manly, fine-looking person, and by many of the fair ones he was called handsome.[9]

New Orleans, near Bowie's new residence, was home to old merchant houses that traded all over Central and South America as well as Europe. The city also served as a base for patriots involved in revolutionary movements for independence that were happening all over the New World. Patriots committed to the independence of Haiti, Venezuela,

Thanks to General Andrew Jackson (seen here) and his success in defeating the British at the Battle of New Orleans, the Bowie brothers' service was not needed in the War of 1812.

Mexico, and many other places bought arms in the local stores and advertised for volunteers in the local newspapers. Walking along the streets of New Orleans, a visitor would hear men conversing, dining, and gambling in several languages.

Jim Bowie frequented the gambling houses of New Orleans and became a knowledgeable gambler, though not always a lucky one.[10] Bowie always had fine manners and was never known to curse.[11] His pleasing speech gave him easy entry into the homes of influential planters and merchants.

Slaves and Texas

It is not recorded when Jim Bowie first visited Texas. He might have gone to Texas to capture wild horses or cattle, which could be sold at an enormous profit in the city of Natchez near his home. If he did not go to Texas for horses or cattle, however, Jim Bowie went there for slaves.

Rezin Pleasant and Jim Bowie would buy slaves at a dollar a pound from the French smuggler and pirate Jean Laffite, who maintained a large slave market on Galveston Island. The Bowie brothers would then take the slaves back to the United States border in Louisiana. At that time, it was illegal to import slaves into Louisiana, although slavery itself was legal. Louisiana law gave anyone who provided information on illegally smuggled slaves one half of the price that the slaves later brought at public auction. When they reached the Louisiana

Jim Bowie developed a sense of courage and enterprise during his early years, growing up on the American frontier.

border, the Bowie brothers would turn in the slaves they had bought from Jean Laffite to the customs agent. Later, they would buy the slaves back cheaply at public auction, while also receiving half that price from the government as their reward. They would then sell the slaves again for a large profit.

The Bowie brothers took their profits from the slave business and bought a plantation they called Arcadia on Bayou Lafourche near Natchez. Rezin Bowie settled down to handle the day-to-day operation of the farm. He became a successful planter. Jim Bowie, however, did not want to settle down and soon moved back to New Orleans.[12]

The Sandbar Knife Fight

Sometime around 1825, when Jim Bowie was trying to finance another of his business schemes, he tried to borrow money from an Alexandria, Louisiana, bank. The sheriff of Rapides Parish, Norris Wright, was both a director of the bank and an enemy of Bowie's. There was a natural dislike between the men. Wright arranged for the bank to deny Bowie the money he needed.

One day, the two men saw each other on the street. Wright pulled out a pistol and shot Jim Bowie in the chest. The bullet knocked down a chair Bowie was holding, but failed to harm him. Bowie's gun, if he had one, misfired. Bowie attacked Wright with his fists and teeth until Wright's friends pulled them apart.

In those days it was a terrible mistake for a man like Jim Bowie to go unarmed. According to legend, Bowie's father or brother Rezin gave him a large knife for protection. On September 19, 1827, on a sandbar on the west side of the Mississippi River, Bowie and five friends met six of Wright's friends for a fight. At first, each side fired their guns until they were empty. Bowie was shot in four places. Norris Wright rushed on the fallen Bowie with a long, thin sword. Bowie rose to one knee and thrust the knife

Bowie Knife

The Bowie knife's size and weight were huge. With over a fourteen-inch blade, it looked like a butcher knife. The top of the blade was thick and straight, the bottom tapered to a fine edge curving gracefully to a point. There was also a heavy horn handle and steel guard to balance the knife, allowing it to be thrown with deadly accuracy.

On the frontier, the Bowie knife was used for skinning game, cutting meat, chopping trees, hammering, fighting, and sometimes picking the teeth. Partly because of Jim Bowie's fame, the knife became the frontier weapon of choice until the six-shooter became popular some ten years later.

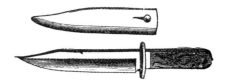

Jim Bowie received a large knife from either his father or brother to use for protection. It later came to be called a Bowie knife.

(which would become famous as the Bowie knife) deep into Wright's heart, killing him. It took Bowie two to three months to recover from his wounds.[13]

Time to Go to Texas

While he was recovering, Bowie must have decided that it was time to move away from Louisiana. Wright had more friends who would be looking to attack him. Although the sandbar fight had been a duel among willing participants and the law usually overlooked such mayhem, Bowie could face possible manslaughter charges for killing Wright. Looking around for a new start, sometime in 1828, Jim Bowie rode into Texas. Bypassing the growing English-speaking settlements in east Texas, he went to San Antonio in the west to seek his fortune as a Mexican citizen.

3

JIM BOWIE SETTLES IN TEXAS

W hen Jim Bowie arrived in San Antonio, it was a town with a population of about fifteen hundred, located in the center of the Mexican state of Coahuila y Texas. Downstream, close to where the San Antonio River emptied into the Gulf of Mexico, was the small town of Goliad.

There were only two other towns in the entire province of Texas: Nacogdoches in north Texas, close to the border with the United States; and San Felipe, a town of less than a hundred people in Stephen F. Austin's new Anglo colony in east Texas. The rest of the vast lands of Texas were dominated by the numerous Indian tribes who lived there. Indians vastly outnumbered the Mexican population of Texas. Many of the citizens of San Antonio and Goliad were Indians themselves.

San Antonio in 1828

San Antonio consisted of a few hundred single-story adobe buildings on the banks of the San Antonio River. The townspeople dug irrigation ditches from the river to their small household gardens, where they grew tomatoes, chilies, corn, and peppers. Most of the town's families also had small ranches in the country, where they kept cattle and horses. It was a good life, but poor and isolated. San Fernando Catholic Church, built from limestone blocks quarried nearby, was the town's largest structure. A quarter of a mile north of the downtown plazas, stood the Alamo mission.

The Alamo mission had been intended to bring the local Indian tribes to Christianity and civilization. The chapel, or church, that we know today as the Alamo was begun in 1758. At that time, there were two rows of adobe houses, a monastery for the Franciscan priests, kitchens, barns, large gardens and orchards, and a weaving room where clothes and blankets were made. By 1785, there were no more Indians to convert. They had either died of disease or intermarried with the local settlers.

Most of the men of San Antonio hunted the wild cattle that roamed on the fertile grassy plains surrounding the town. The principal source of cash in the town was the salary of the Mexican soldiers stationed at the local fort. Their salaries were often six months late arriving from Mexico City, and there were times when there simply was no cash in the town. Everyone dealt by barter and with credit from the local merchants.

Because almost everyone in town was in debt, people learned to enjoy themselves without money. Parties and dances were free, often, and open to all of the leading families in town. The many religious festivals each year were paid for by the church and provided popular entertainment for all.

Americans in Texas

When Jim Bowie came to Texas, he did not settle with the new Austin colony of Americans who lived there already. Moses Austin had obtained permission from the Mexican government in 1821 to settle American families in Texas. He died before he could settle any colonists in Texas, but his son, Stephen F. Austin, continued his father's work. By the time Jim Bowie came to Texas, Austin's colony numbered several thousand people and was thriving in the fertile and well-watered lands east of San Antonio. When Bowie came to Texas, however, he did not linger in the company of other Americans. He traveled immediately on to San Antonio.

Bowie Joins the Catholic Church

The first public record of Jim Bowie in San Antonio is on June 26, 1828. According to Mexican law, it

Stephen Fuller Austin founded an Anglo colony in the Mexican province of Texas, east of San Antonio.

was necessary to be a member of the Roman Catholic Church to become a Mexican citizen, and it was necessary to be a citizen of Mexico to do business. If Jim Bowie were serious about leaving the United States, he would have to be a member of the Catholic Church in order to make a living. On June 26, 1828, the priest of the town, whose knowledge of the details of Bowie's life was clearly limited, wrote:

> I, the priest, Refugio de la Garza, proper pastor of this City, having proceeded with the necessary instruction in catechism proscribed by the Roman Ritual, solemnly baptized and put the holy oils and chrism to James Bowie, twenty-three years old, born in South Carolina, legal son of James Bowie and Jane Bowie.[1]

Bowie's sponsors were Juan Martín de Veramendi and his wife, Josefa Navarro. To be one's sponsor at baptism is an honor among friends. It appears that there was already a close friendship between Jim Bowie and Juan Martín de Veramendi when Bowie first came to town. Veramendi had been one of the exiled Mexican revolutionaries in New Orleans at the same time Jim Bowie was living there.

Bowie's Influential Mexican Friend

Juan Martín de Veramendi had been born in San Antonio on December 17, 1778. His family had been prominent in Spain years before. They were called "Castilian" because of their pure Spanish heritage. The family worked hard to establish a

Bowie's baptism at this font inside San Fernando Church is the first record of his time in Texas.

The Mexican Revolution From Spain

On September 16, 1810, Father Miguel Hidalgo gathered hundreds of his Indian parishioners around him. They seized the local town of Dolores in an effort to free Mexico from Spanish rule. Soon, hundreds of thousands of Indians joined him. Hidalgo's army was defeated early in 1811, and he was captured and executed in August.

The goal of Mexican independence, however, did not die with Hidalgo. For the next ten years, various revolutionary leaders continued the bloody war, until finally, on July 18, 1821, Spanish troops submitted to revolutionary General Agustín de Iturbide, who proclaimed himself Emperor Agustín I. In 1823, Antonio López de Santa Anna led a successful revolt against him that resulted in the creation of a democracy under the Mexican Federal Constitution of 1824.

merchant business between San Antonio and Goliad, the other Spanish town in Texas. Young Juan Martín married Josefa Navarro, the daughter of two of the town's leading republican families, the Seguíns and the Navarros. The families of Juan Martín de Veramendi, Erasmo Seguín, and José Antonio Navarro were hard hit after a defeat of the revolutionaries in 1813. These men all fled to the United States after the disastrous battle.[2] But now these families were the leading politicians and civic leaders of San Antonio.

Erasmo Seguín and Juan Martín de Veramendi had met Stephen F. Austin on June 21, 1821, when he first came to Texas. They accompanied him to San Antonio. These men used their influence to aid Austin's efforts. In return, they became rich from their association with the American colonists. Each of these families had stores where they sold thread, cloth, and other items. They also sold horses and cattle. Another thing that the San Antonio merchants could sell to the new immigrants was land.

Bowie Becomes a Mexican Citizen

In the fall of 1830, Jim Bowie and Juan Martín de Veramendi traveled from San Antonio to Saltillo, the capital city of the state. At the regular session of the state legislature, Juan Martín Veramendi proposed to make Jim Bowie a citizen of Mexico. The whole legislature passed the measure on October 5, 1830. The decree that made Jim Bowie a Mexican citizen stated that Bowie would be required to open a cotton and wool cloth factory in Saltillo, which would not be required to pay any taxes for a period of twenty years. The members of the legislature welcomed Jim Bowie as a Mexican citizen and wished him well.[3]

The Land Business

By law, only Mexican citizens could own land in Texas. Stephen F. Austin's grant from the Mexican government to settle foreign colonists in Texas was an exception to this rule. His grant gave him the right to assign land titles to his colonists. Each family in Austin's colony was entitled to receive a square mile of land. Other American settlers in Texas outside of Austin's colony had no legal right to the land they lived on. However, it was easy for Mexican citizens to buy huge parcels of vacant land in Texas from the state government under very friendly terms. It was possible to buy eleven square miles of land at one time, a little less than fifty thousand acres. The price of this land was about four cents an acre. No payment was required for the first three years. Thereafter, three yearly payments were required to pay the total amount due.

Bowie probably went into the land business with Juan Martín de Veramendi as soon as he arrived in Texas. Veramendi had applied for and was granted title to an eleven-square-mile piece of Texas land years before Bowie came to Texas.[4] Bowie himself began to speculate in land in Texas in 1830 and again in 1831.[5]

Veramendi Becomes Vice Governor

Juan Martín de Veramendi soon became an important figure in local politics. Later in the same session of the legislature that had given Jim Bowie Mexican citizenship, José María de Letona from Saltillo was elected governor of the state of Coahuila y Texas. The election for vice governor resulted in a tie between Ignacio de Arizpe of Saltillo and Juan Martín de Veramendi. In order to break the tie, the legislature voted on January 4, 1831, electing Veramendi.[6]

This election began a significant change in the life of Juan Martín de Veramendi. In November 1831, he moved his family to Saltillo from San Antonio. Among the family members on the week-long trip was his eighteen-year-old daughter, Ursula. One of the men from San Antonio who accompanied the new vice governor to Saltillo was Jim Bowie, now thirty-four.[7] Bowie and Ursula must have known each other for a few years, but a close family friend said that it was on this trip that the couple first flirted over the campfires at night and fell in love.

Love and Marriage

Bowie married Ursula Veramendi in San Antonio on April 22, 1831. The same priest who had baptized him wrote in the church records:

> I, the priest, Rev. Refugio de la Garza, the proper pastor of the City, . . . married and veiled in the face of the Church, Mr. James Bowie, a native of Louisiana of North America, legal son of Mr. Ramon Bowie and Mrs. Alvina Jones; to Miss Ursula de Veramendi, a native of this said City, legal daughter of Mr. Juan Martín de Veramendi and Mrs. Maria Josepha Navarro.[8]

When the newly married couple left the religious ceremony at San Fernando Church, Bowie proceeded across the main plaza to the mayor's office. In another ceremony, this time a civil (nonreligious) declaration of their union, Jim Bowie swore to make a legally binding gift to his new bride:

> In view of the virtue, honesty and other laudable gifts with which his future spouse is adorned, he [James Bowie] offers her as an augment of the dowry, or as an Aras or pre-nuptial present, on account of the nuptials, according as it may be useful in case the concerted marriage should be realized, the quantity of $15,000 which are drawn from the most select of his estate or property.[9]

In a document filed with the city, Jim Bowie's property was listed. He owned land in Arkansas, Louisiana, and Texas. His prenuptial agreement deeded to Ursula the machinery for the cotton mills in Saltillo that had been purchased already but were still in the factory in Boston. They were valued at $20,000. Bowie estimated his financial worth at that time at $220,000.[10]

Despite his financial assets, however, Bowie was always in need of cash. He was not poor, and he lived well, but he probably spent all the cash he could get as quickly as he could get it. Bowie and his brothers did own a substantial plantation near Natchez, and he had titles to many acres in the wilderness of Arkansas and Texas. But when Bowie estimated the value of these properties, he had no one ready to buy them. The value was all speculation. He bought the land very cheaply and hoped to sell it in the future for what he estimated on the day of his wedding.

Jim Bowie married Ursula Veramendi at the San Fernando Church (seen here as it looks today) on April 22, 1831.

Bowie and Ursula's wedding was the best show seen in San Antonio for a long time. The event was the talk of the town, if not all of Texas. The party after the wedding lasted a week, moving from home to home in a series of dinners and dances.[11]

Jim and Ursula Bowie then made a honeymoon trip to New Orleans and the nearby towns of Louisiana, where his mother, Elve, and all the other Bowies met the beautiful young bride. When the couple returned to Texas in late June 1831, the newlyweds brought both brother Rezin and several carts full of trade goods Jim Bowie had purchased in New Orleans to sell in San Antonio at the Veramendi general store downtown.[12]

4

INDIAN FIGHTER

T he newlyweds set up housekeeping in San Antonio at the home of Juan Martín de Veramendi. They enjoyed an idyllic life during the next few years. It was fun and exciting. According to the reports of all who saw them, they were devoted to each other.

Jim Bowie, however, was away from home often, hunting treasure, hunting Indians, and hunting land. One of the most entertaining pastimes for the young men of the town was searching for the silver mines and gold deposits rumored (falsely) to be nearby.

Indians and Silver

One band of Lipan Apache, who lived near San Antonio, was led by a chief named Xolic. Once or twice every year, Xolic led the men of his tribe into San Antonio to obtain blankets, steel knives, needles, and other goods. Xolic always paid for these goods with small silver nuggets that had flakes of gold in them. The Lipan would never tell where the nuggets came from. It was rumored that the Lipan men had pledged that whoever revealed the source of the silver would be tortured to death. Soon the local residents gave up trying to find out the location of the silver. But Jim Bowie heard the rumors of the Indian silver, and he and his brother Rezin determined to try their luck at finding it.

Soon after Jim and Ursula Bowie returned from their honeymoon, Bowie and Rezin left San Antonio with a small party of eight friends in search of the Indian silver.[1] Two members of the party were young boys who would tend the horses and find firewood for the rest. In the story of their adventure, as the two Bowie brothers later told it, not much happened right away.

Fighting Indians

For two weeks, the men searched the countryside without luck. On the morning of November 19, 1831, the Bowie party met two Comanche Indians and a captive Mexican on the Bandera Road, about a hundred miles northwest of San Antonio. The newcomers dismounted, and they all exchanged small tokens, presents of tobacco and gunpowder. They talked for about an hour.

The Mexican prisoner, acting as a translator, informed the Bowie party that the Indians belonged to a party of sixteen warriors under the command of Chief Isaonie. They were returning some horses to San Antonio that had been stolen shortly before by braves of the Waco and Tonkawa tribe. After the theft, the Indians had driven the stolen horses northwest into Comanche territory. Meeting the horse thieves, the Comanche had stolen back the horses. Chief Isaonie was driving the horses back to San Antonio in the hope of receiving a reward. The Indians wanted to know if it would be safe for them to enter San Antonio. Bowie assured them that they would not be attacked. The Indian party soon left, and the Bowie party returned to exploring.

The next morning, the Mexican captive they had met the day before rode into Bowie's camp. His horse had evidently run all night. The Mexican said he had been sent back by Chief Isaonie to tell Bowie's party that they were being stalked by another group, a war party made up of more than one hundred fifty Indians. The war party had met Chief Isaonie the evening before and had invited the Comanche to join them in their fight. Chief Isaonie had refused. After they left, he sent the Mexican captive to warn Bowie.

Bowie and his men mounted their horses and headed for a deserted Spanish fort located along the San Saba River, to the west. They rode all day, but failed to reach the fort before dark. They camped for the night in a thick grove of oak trees. This cluster of thirty to forty trees was surrounded by a dense thicket of brambles, bushes, and saplings. Close to the grove was a stream. All around lay open prairie with some limestone hills in the distance. Before settling in for the night, the men cut a path inside the thick bushes, ten feet from the outer edge all around. They cleared away the cactus in the path, brought all the horses and supplies into the inner clearing, and posted guards to watch for the Indians. Their careful preparation would save their lives.

The Attack

The next morning, as the men got ready to move on to the San Saba fort, they suddenly saw Indians about two hundred yards to the east, following their trail. In front of the main body, only about a hundred yards from the live oak thicket, a single warrior walked bent over, stalking. He had not yet seen Bowie's position.

The men reached for their rifles. They dismounted and quickly tied their horses and pack animals to the trees in the center of their defensive position. When the Indians saw where the Bowie party had dug in, they retreated out of rifle range and began to get ready for battle. The Bowie party could see that they were indeed outnumbered by more than fifteen to one. They decided to try to talk their way out.

Rezin Bowie and David Buchanan walked to within about forty yards of the Indian position. They called out, requesting a meeting with the chief. Their answer was a screech from the Indians, followed by about twelve rifle shots. One of the balls of lead broke Buchanan's leg. Rezin fired back with his double-barreled shotgun, quickly hoisted Buchanan over his shoulder, and ran back to the thicket. The rest of the party started firing their rifles to cover the retreat. On the way back to the thicket, Buchanan was wounded twice more, and several bullets tore holes in Rezin Bowie's shirt without causing him any injury. Eight of the Indians ran after the slowly retreating men, but four of them were shot dead by the men in the thicket. The other four quickly returned to the Indian position out of range of the deadly accurate aim of the defenders.

One large party of Indians took cover in the rocks of a limestone hill to the northeast of the oak thicket, about fifty yards away. They began shooting, but because they could not see the men hidden by the thick bushes, their fire was ineffective.

One of the Indian leaders was mounted on a horse and calmly walked among the rocks, in plain sight of the defenders, encouraging his men to make an assault on the thicket. Caiaphas Ham took careful aim, shooting the Indian through the leg and killing his horse. The Indian fell to the ground, jumped up, and began hopping around with his war shield held up toward the defenders, again urging his men to make an assault on the Bowie party. Immediately, four bullets tore through the shield, and the brave Indian fell dead. Six to eight Indians ran out of hiding to recover their fallen chief. Four of them were shot before they could remove the body.

The Indians retreated behind the hill, but soon returned and poured a heavy fire of rifle balls and arrows into the thicket. Again, they were directed by a war chief mounted on a horse. This time it was Jim Bowie who shot the chief from his horse, and again, the Indians lost several men as they recovered the body of their leader. The whole battle so far had lasted no more than fifteen or twenty minutes.

During this short but intense rifle battle, twenty or so Indians moved to the bank of the nearby stream where they had a much better view of the defending party. They began firing into the thicket and soon wounded Matthew Doyle, the rifle ball entering his left breast and exiting through his back. When Doyle cried out that he was wounded, Thomas McCaslin rushed to the spot where Doyle had been shot and stood up to get a clear shot at an Indian he saw. McCaslin was shot through the center of his body and died instantly. Another of the defenders, Robert Armstrong, stood up and another Indian shot rang out that broke the stock of Armstrong's rifle. Armstrong quickly dove to the ground. Never again did the men of the Bowie party show such dangerous emotion or stupidity.

Indians now completely surrounded the thicket and continued to fire into it well into the afternoon. The great advantage of the defenders was that the Indians could not see them. As soon as one of the defenders fired his rifle, he moved six or eight feet to either side. The Indians would then fire through the bushes where they had seen the smoke of the rifle shot, but the defender would no longer be there. In this way, the battle continued for more than two hours.

The Battle Continues

The Indians next decided to try to dislodge the Bowie party from their strong defensive position. They set fire to the dead grass of the prairie upwind of the oak grove. When Bowie saw the Indians' strategy, he moved the wounded into the center of the grove of trees. He then had two young boys gather rocks and baggage to build a small wall around the wounded men. The boys then swept the area clear of dead grass and branches. Under cover of the advancing smoke and fire, the Indians recovered the bodies of their wounded and dead, but their strategy failed as the wind shifted direction and the fire swept around the oak thicket, leaving the Bowie party's defensive position untouched.

About four in the afternoon, the Indians set fire to the unburned grass near the camp. This time the

Bowie and his men used muzzle-loading long rifles like these in their battle with the Indians.

fire penetrated the thicket. The defenders used their blankets and buffalo robes to smother the flames. Although the fire did little damage to either the oak trees or the makeshift breastwork of the defenders, it did burn away the bushes and brambles that had hidden the men from their Indian attackers. All the defenders moved to the center of the grove and formed a circle around the wounded. They were determined to fight to the end.

But the Indians never came. The battle, which had lasted over thirteen hours, was over. Bowie and his men had suffered one dead and three wounded, along with five horses killed and three wounded. The estimated Indian casualties were forty dead and forty-two wounded. The Indians retreated out of range and began to mourn their dead and treat the wounded. All night long, the Indian campfires burned brightly as they danced and cried in tribute to their fallen comrades. The next morning, there were no Indians to be seen. For eight days, Bowie's group stayed in camp, tending to the wounded, afraid of an Indian trap if they left their defensive position.

On the evening of November 29, the Bowie party loaded its wounded onto its few remaining horses and started to walk back to San Antonio. They walked southeast to the Pedernales River, where they saw signs of several large Tonkawa war parties. They reversed course. For the next week, they walked south, finally turning east after they had crossed the Guadalupe River, thirty miles northwest of San Antonio. On December 6, the men finally returned to San Antonio.[2]

The men must have told the tale of the fight with good cheer. It certainly seemed to cause Bowie little concern. Captain William G. Hunt recalled that he met Jim and Ursula Bowie at a party on Christmas Day, 1831, in one of the settlements along the Colorado River. Hunt later wrote: "Mrs. Bowie was a beautiful Castilian lady, and won all hearts by her sweet manners. Bowie was supremely happy with her, very devoted and more like a kind and tender lover than the terrible duelist he has *since* been represented to be."[3]

Hunting the Renegade Indians

Early in 1832, Jim Bowie mounted an unsuccessful expedition against the Indians who had attacked him. Bowie claimed that they had several thousand horses that were worth catching. The rumor spread that Jim Bowie was simply looking for buried treasure again. On January 10, 1832, Bowie took out an advertisement in the *Texas Gazette* insisting that he was planning a legitimate Indian raid. The particularly guilty Indians must have heard that Bowie was coming after them, because in a tour of several hundred miles around San Antonio, Bowie never saw a single Indian.[4]

It appears that Jim Bowie spent part of the spring of 1832 in Austin's colonies.[5] In June, his brother Stephen and a friend, Edwin Moorhouse, visited the Bowies in San Antonio.[6] Jim Bowie left Texas soon after, perhaps to escort his brother back to Louisiana. When he returned to Texas at the beginning of August 1832, changes were beginning to happen that would dramatically affect Bowie's life.

Changing Times

In 1832, Mexican Army troops were sent to three places in east Texas to try and stop the many illegal squatters, smugglers, and adventurers who were coming to Texas from the United States. Army posts were established at Nacogdoches, Anahuac, at the mouth of the Trinity River, and at Velasco, at the mouth of the Brazos River. Of course, the illegal immigrants resented the presence of Mexican Army troops, but the legal residents in Austin's colony also looked at the Mexican soldiers with distrust. The closest government post had been in San Antonio. The only authority in east Texas had been Stephen F. Austin. If there were any trouble in the colony, Austin and the officials in San Antonio decided what to do. The colonists liked this arrangement just fine. The authorities in Mexico City, however, decided to station regular army units in the area to maintain order. In each locality where Mexican troops were stationed, there was trouble.

In late July 1832, the civil authorities of Nacogdoches agreed to join with groups of men from the surrounding areas to compel the Mexican force stationed in town to leave. About three hundred men approached and surrounded the town on August 1. All the civilians quickly left.

The rebels informed the Mexican commander, Colonel José de las Piedras, of their intentions. He chose to fight rather than retreat. At noon on August 2, the rebels marched to the center of town. Suddenly, about one hundred Mexican cavalrymen assaulted them and fired a volley. The alcalde (mayor) of the town was killed. The rebels returned fire and took cover in the houses that fronted the town square. There was firing all afternoon. In the evening, the Mexican troops mounted an assault on the square. They were repulsed by the rebels with heavy fire from the windows of the houses on the town square.

During the night, Colonel Piedras retreated from town, leaving behind his dead and wounded soldiers. He refused to surrender but turned over official command of the Mexican force to Major Francisco Medina, who immediately surrendered with over three hundred men. Colonel James W. Bullock, the commander of the rebel force, did not know what to do with the prisoners. He could not simply turn them loose, yet none of his men wanted to take them all the way to San Antonio, the closest army post.

Jim Bowie rode into Nacogdoches on his way home to San Antonio. He talked with Colonel

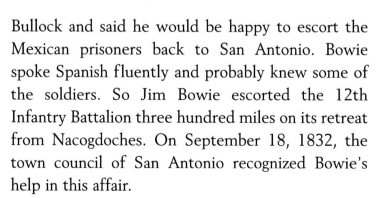

The Government of Coahuila y Texas

In 1830 the state legislature of Coahuila y Texas contained only eleven representatives. They had been elected to their positions by the voters of the five districts of the state: Saltillo, Parras, Monclova, Texas, and Rio Grande. Saltillo, Parras, and Monclova were the largest cities of the state; they each had three representatives. The whole state of Texas had one representative, and the cluster of towns along the Rio Grande had one. In 1831 the state legislature gave Texas another vote, when the district of Nacogdoches was created. Enough colonists from the United States had established legal residence there to justify another representative. In 1834, Texas received another representative because of the further increase of colonists. So, the political fate of Texas from 1830 to 1836 was controlled by only eleven, twelve, or thirteen men.

Bullock and said he would be happy to escort the Mexican prisoners back to San Antonio. Bowie spoke Spanish fluently and probably knew some of the soldiers. So Jim Bowie escorted the 12th Infantry Battalion three hundred miles on its retreat from Nacogdoches. On September 18, 1832, the town council of San Antonio recognized Bowie's help in this affair.

For the next two years, there was no Mexican governmental authority present among the new colonists in east Texas. As the number of American colonists grew in Texas, many cried out against the laws of Mexico, even though these laws were not observed or enforced. Naturally, the Mexican authorities found the American colonists ungrateful. After all, they paid no taxes and they were growing rich in the fertile river valleys of east Texas. Very soon, the distrust between the Mexican government and the Texas colonists would grow into hostility.

5

POLITICAL DYNASTY AND TRAGEDY

On October 14, 1832, Governor Letona of Coahuila y Texas died.[1] The state legislature called for Vice Governor Juan Martín de Veramendi to assume executive powers at the next session of the legislature that was scheduled to meet on January 1, 1833, in Saltillo.[2]

The death of Governor Letona must have appeared as a divine favor to the leaders of San Antonio. Letona was a native of Saltillo, the largest city in the state. It had a larger population than all of Texas, both Anglos and Mexicans combined.

As in all political situations, there was a party of the "haves" and the "have nots" in the state. The "haves" were the representatives from the

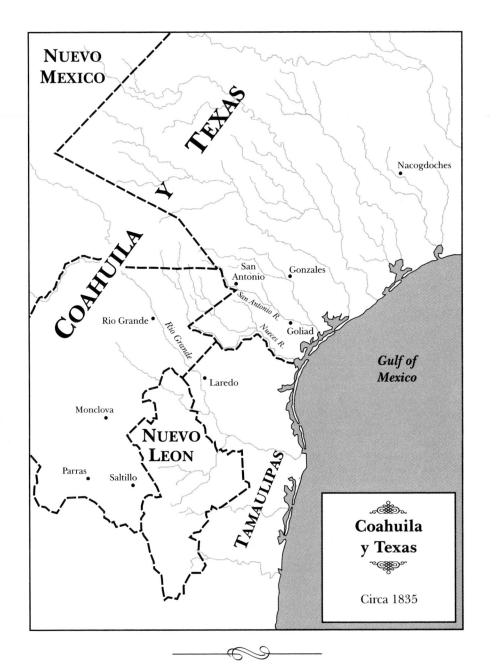

The province of Coahuila y Texas was divided between the wealthy residents of Saltillo and Parras and the people of areas like Monclova and Rio Grande.

departments of Saltillo and Parras. For years, the politicians of Saltillo and Parras had used this majority to elect the governor they wanted and to pass laws that helped their friends. They ignored the needs of Texas, as well as the needs of the other departments of the state, Monclova and Rio Grande.

The Viesca Brothers

The most influential politicians from Parras were the Viesca brothers, Agustín and José María. José María Viesca had helped write the Mexican constitution in 1824, which had given most of the power in the country to the states rather than the national government. He had also served as the first governor of Coahuila y Texas under that constitution. Agustín had been the minister of relations in Mexico City under the presidency of Vincente Guerrero. Both Viesca brothers ardently supported the principles of the federal constitution. When the politicians of Saltillo began to support the movement to give more power to the national government, a deep hatred developed between these former political allies.

The Politicians of San Antonio Search for New Allies

A simple majority of the state legislature was needed along with the governor's approval to pass a law, but a two-thirds majority was needed to pass a law over the veto of the governor.[3] By himself, Governor Veramendi could veto any law passed by the legislature, and he could pass any emergency laws that were necessary when the legislature was not in session. But he and the other representatives from San Antonio could not pass any regular law they wanted without the approval of the majority of the other legislators. It was time for San Antonio politicians to seek new friends among the other legislators in the halls of Congress in Saltillo. There is good reason to believe that the civic leaders in San Antonio did just that. There is also evidence that Jim Bowie went to Washington, D.C., to talk to the political leaders there about support for Governor Veramendi and the Mexican leaders in San Antonio.

Jim Bowie Goes to Washington

In late November or early December 1832, Jim Bowie was on the Cumberland stagecoach somewhere between Wheeling, now in West Virginia, and Washington, D.C. William McGinley, who was riding the stage, remembered meeting Bowie. McGinley was riding with four other passengers: a young girl, a stranger smoking a large pipe, statesman Henry Clay, and another stranger who sat in a corner with a coat pulled up around his face, apparently lost in thought. The stranger with the pipe soon had the coach filled with thick clouds of tobacco smoke. The young girl began to cough and leaned forward to ask the pipe smoker to stop. The smoker replied that he had paid his fare and would do as he pleased. McGinley later wrote:

The words were no sooner out of his mouth than my seatmate sprang up, threw aside his cloak, and drew from the back of his neck a wicked-looking knife, *the worst I had ever seen.* He quickly seized the smoker by the chin, and, snapping his head back, placed the blade of the knife at his throat, saying: "I will give you just one minute to throw that thing out of the window!" Needless to say, this was done, upon which my seatmate resumed his place, and again pulled the greatcoat about his face. At the next stage stand, Mr. Clay and I introduced ourselves to the stranger, and learned that he was James Bowie.[4]

While Bowie was in Washington, D.C., that winter, he met Archibald Hotchkiss, a Texas colonist, who described Bowie as "a splendid man in appearance, with intelligence and energy strongly marked on his face."[5]

Jim Bowie and Sam Houston Meet in Texas

Whatever business Jim Bowie had in Washington, he concluded it quickly. He returned to Texas three weeks later for Christmas dinner in Stephen F. Austin's colony at San Felipe. While he was there, he met Sam Houston, the ex-governor of Tennessee, who had come to Texas at the request of President Andrew Jackson of the United States to investigate conditions there. They rode on to San Antonio together.[6]

Jim Bowie introduced Houston to his family and friends in San Antonio. Houston had several long interviews with the leading families of San Antonio. No one ever admitted that Houston had come to San

Antonio because of Jim Bowie's trip to Washington. However, Sam Houston soon thereafter wrote a long letter about his experiences in San Antonio to President Jackson, in which he sympathetically presented the position of the people of San Antonio.[7]

Jim Bowie Goes to Mexico

Jim Bowie traveled to Saltillo in the first days of January 1833 with a party of seven Americans. He arrived on February 7. Bowie proposed to the politicians from Parras and Monclova that they band together with Governor Veramendi and the legislators from San Antonio to form a new voting majority that would take the power away from the politicians of Saltillo. The leaders agreed.

On March 9, 1833, the state legislature passed a decree that moved the capital of the state of Coahuila y Texas to Monclova from Saltillo. The new law required all state legislators to live there and to be present on the first of April.[8] This was the public announcement that there was a new majority in the state, and it was a direct slap in the face to the politicians of Saltillo. It was reported that the citizens of Saltillo were so angry over the loss of their power that they rose up as a mob and ran all the legislators out of town.[9]

Success

Bowie returned to Texas sometime after March 9, 1833. During the regular legislative sessions in the spring and fall of 1833, the new legislature in Monclova made laws. Governor Veramendi and the representatives showed that they understood the needs and wants of the Anglo colonists by passing a number of measures that Stephen F. Austin and other Anglo colonists had specifically requested. The law forbidding foreign-born citizens from participating in business was repealed on April 3, 1833. The use of the English language in official documents was allowed in Texas as of March 18, 1834. The state of Coahuila y Texas approved a judicial code for use in Texas that was very similar to English and American traditions: trial by a jury of peers and an appellate court under a supreme court were established on May 5, 1834.

Tragedy Strikes

The Veramendi family moved to Monclova and continued to do a lucrative mercantile business from there. In June 1833, Bowie urged his wife to join her parents in Monclova for the summer. He had plans to be away from San Antonio and wanted her to be with relatives. Besides, Monclova, located high in the mountains, is cooler in the summer than San Antonio.

Early that fall, a cholera epidemic swept through Monclova and killed Governor Juan Martín de Veramendi, his wife Josefa Navarro, and their daughter, Ursula Bowie. They all became ill and died within three days in September.[10] On September 26,

1833, José Antonio Navarro wrote Samuel M. Williams of the death of the governor and his family:

> I have lost a very loyal brother-in-law in Veramendi, and Texas a good son, a faithful and interested friend. Texas is now a political orphan in the government of the state. . . . Three days illness were enough—from the 5th to the 8th of this month—to end all these precious lives. In fact during the first 18 days of this month 571 persons died in Monclova. . . . Poor Bowie is now a widower. I wish you would in some way advise him of this sad news.[11]

Bowie was in Natchez, Mississippi, in October 1833, when he received the word of the death of Ursula and the rest of the Veramendi family.[12] In one stroke, Jim Bowie learned that he had lost his beloved young wife and his good friend and business partner, the governor of the state.

Two State Governments

The death of Governor Veramendi marked the end of the leadership of the state government by the families of San Antonio. In Monclova, the Viesca brothers from Parras continued to run the government of the state. They arranged the emergency appointment of one of their friends to finish Governor Veramendi's term in office. The representatives from San Antonio and Monclova continued to support the new governor. Of course, the politicians of Saltillo were outraged. They saw a chance to get back the governorship and move the capital back to Saltillo. They elected one of their friends, a member of the state supreme court, as governor and claimed to be the legitimate government of the state, based once again in Saltillo. Both governments quickly spent all of their available money on soldiers, arms, and military supplies. In July and August 1834, there were cavalry battles between the militias of Monclova and Saltillo on the vast desert plateau that separated the two cities. Jim Bowie fought on the side of Monclova in these battles.[13] No one won the battles, and both sides sought more money and more troops.

Most of the money in the state was controlled by the politicians of Saltillo. The big factories and stores in the state were located there and most of the tax revenue was paid there. The politicians of Saltillo used this money to finance their state government. The government in Monclova had no real income if it did not receive tax money from the state's largest city, Saltillo. With the representatives from Saltillo in revolt and protected by an armed militia, there was no income. The government in Monclova began to sell hundreds of square miles of land in Texas to speculators at very cheap prices, but always in cash. They spent that money on their army.

Texas Land

Until Jim Bowie's arrival in Texas, there seemed to be little desire on the part of private Mexican citizens for Texas land. From this time on, however, the buying and selling of land became a lucrative business.

Land speculators would prompt Mexican citizens to apply for grants of land from the government. These speculators, in turn, would sell the grants to other land speculators in Mexico, Texas, and the United States. Bowie could sell the Texas land grants to his friends in New Orleans and Natchez. He was not the only, or the biggest, dealer in Texas land.

The Monclova government started to sell land, too. The Galveston Bay and Texas Land Company was formed in New York in 1830. It purchased an interest in millions of acres of Texas land. Although the company did send a few settlers to Texas, its main purpose was to buy Texas land. It was a grand land speculation—buying cheap, selling dear. They could always sell the land to new settlers in Mexican Texas, but if Texas gained its independence from Mexico and became a part of the United States, the value of the land owned by the company would increase enormously. The Galveston Bay Company hired agents in Texas and Mexico to act for them in the local legislatures and courts. In 1832, Sam Houston was considered but did not get the job. Jim Bowie was given the job in 1834. Through a number of agents, the Galveston Bay Company began to pay large sums of money to the government in Monclova for huge plots of Texas land, up to four hundred square miles at a time.

Jim Bowie had great influence with the government in Monclova and was made a land commissioner by the legislature. In this way, Bowie, acting as both a state official and an agent of the Galveston Bay and Texas Land Company, could simply transfer the title to Texas lands to the agents of the company. From February to November 1835, Bowie, as the state land commissioner, signed the title for ninety-five square miles of Texas land. He signed blank titles that were filled in and dated later.[14]

Most of the small landholders in Texas came to look on the government in Monclova with suspicion. Small families who had settled in Texas without official permission had been trying unsuccessfully for years to get a title to the lands they were farming. They saw millions of acres being deeded to rich people in New York who had never even seen Texas. They felt that the politicians in Monclova were lining their own pockets unfairly. They were probably right. Bowie and the rest of the land speculators, including many in the government, saw these land deals only as a good business. There was a bigger picture that most of these settlers and land dealers did not see.

The Dictatorship of General Santa Anna

General Antonio López de Santa Anna, the president of Mexico, was trying to take away from the states of Mexico the considerable freedoms and rights that had been given to them by the constitution of 1824. When Santa Anna had been elected, the presidency of Mexico was mostly a ceremonial position. Almost all the power of government rested in the individual states. They could raise their own armies and pass their own laws.

Santa Anna wanted to bring all the power of government under his control. He wanted to be a dictator. He had recently sent a large army into the state of Zacatecas and defeated a state militia of ten thousand Zacatecans. He then allowed his army to burn the city of Zacatecas and steal everything of value. All the other states in Mexico quickly submitted to Santa Anna's demands except Coahuila y Texas. The government in Monclova defied Santa Anna and defended the federalist principles of the constitution of 1824. The Saltillo government backed Santa Anna and asked him to send his army into their state to defeat the federalists in Monclova.

Santa Anna told the federalists to stop selling the public land in Texas. They told him to mind his own business. Santa Anna appointed his brother-in-law, General Martín Perfecto de Cos, commander of the northern region of Mexico that included Coahuila y Texas. He planned to use soldiers to enforce his will. The federalists continued to sell the public lands of Texas to investors in the United States and use the money to hire soldiers and buy horses and rifles.

Santa Anna Moves Against the Federalists

Santa Anna finally ordered General Cos to arrest the members of the federalist government in Monclova. Rather than fight there, the federalists planned to escape across the Rio Grande and continue the fight

General Antonio López de Santa Anna, as president of Mexico, tried to take away people's constitutional rights and set himself up as the dictator of the nation.

against Santa Anna from San Antonio. When General Cos's troops reached Monclova in May 1835, all of the state legislators and visiting land agents had mounted their horses and made a run for the Rio Grande.

The new governor, Agustín Viesca, took the archives of the state, which included all the land titles, and followed the rest of the legislature away from Monclova two or three days later. He had stayed behind because he was waiting for Jim Bowie and General John Thomson Mason, an agent of the Galveston Bay and Texas Land Company, to return

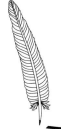

The Arrival of General Cos

On September 20, 1835, Colonel James Power watched a warship pass into Copano Bay. Soon, five hundred Mexican soldiers and supplies were being unloaded. The commanding officer of the troops was General Cos himself. Cos greeted Colonel Power. He said he had come to silence protesters. General Cos showed Power a copy of a proclamation:

> I make known to all and every one of the inhabitants of the three departments of Texas, that whenever . . . any should attempt to disturb the public order and peace, that the inevitable consequences of the war will bear upon them and their property. . . .

Cos asked Power what he thought. Power replied, "I think it would have been better had you not come."[15]

from Matamoros with forty thousand dollars as a final land payment on one of their deals.[16]

After Bowie and Mason delivered the land payment to Governor Viesca in Monclova on May 23, 1835, they probably returned to Matamoros. Jim Bowie left Matamoros on June 12. General Cos had forbidden all foreigners to leave the city. He had closed the port to regular ship traffic and cut off civilian mail service to and from Texas. This was probably not much of a problem for Bowie. He just swam his horse across the Rio Grande and rode along the seacoast to friendly settlements two hundred miles away.

In July, Jim Bowie went to east Texas. He visited the Shawnee and Cherokee Indian settlements and sought their help in the coming struggle against Santa Anna.[17] He then traveled back to the Bowie family plantation near Natchez and convinced some of his friends there to invest in some land in Texas. Bowie returned to Texas in the company of Angus McNeil of Mississippi and Dr. William Richardson. They brought eighty thousand dollars for land deals. But by the time they got back, there was no federalist government left to deal with.[18]

The Defeat of the Federalist Government

When Governor Viesca finally received the forty thousand dollars for the land payment, he rallied a large body of militia from San Antonio under the command of Juan Seguín and rode for San Antonio.

He encountered a party of General Cos's cavalry and refused to fight them. He retreated back to Monclova, minus the land records and the money. His militia thought he was a coward and deserted him. Viesca changed his mind a few days later and escaped across the deserts of south Texas. He showed up in Goliad after the Texans had seized the fort. The Texan forces did not recognize Governor Viesca as their lawful Commander in Chief. Viesca was sent to the new revolutionary government of Texas where he was again treated as a refugee rather than the lawful head of state. This ended the federalist government. Those Texans who wanted to continue to fight the dictatorship of General Santa Anna now joined the Texan Army.

6

EARLY CONFLICTS OF THE TEXAS REVOLUTION

On September 20, 1835, General Cos landed on the Texas coast with five hundred troops. He had come to arrest the federalist leaders and discipline the Anglo colonists. The news of Cos's arrival spread all over Texas within a few days. Some Texans saw Cos's arrival as the first act in a war for the independence of Texas. Some saw it as an opportunity to capture the gold he was rumored to be carrying. Whatever their motives, almost every man in Texas took up a rifle and headed for the action.

Battle of Gonzales

The first battle of the war in Texas came in Gonzales. The settlers there refused to return a small cannon that had been given to them by the Mexican forces in San Antonio to fight off Indian attacks. The cannon had never been used, but when the commander of the Mexican Army in San Antonio sent a company of soldiers to retrieve it, the colonists told them to "Come and Take It."[1] For several days they talked, the Mexicans on one side of the Guadalupe River and the colonists on the other, while the men in Gonzales appealed to the rest of Texas for support.

On October 2, there were more than one hundred fifty volunteers from all over Texas gathered, ready for a fight. They filled the cannon with chains and scrap iron, crossed the river, and fired on the Mexicans. One Mexican soldier was killed. The Mexican troops retreated to San Antonio. The firing of the cannon and the death of a soldier were irrevocable acts of war.[2] The colonists knew it and began to march toward San Antonio, sixty miles away.

Battle of Goliad

At the same time as the call went out to support the men at Gonzales, several groups of colonists decided to attack General Cos directly where he had stopped on his march inland, at the fort at Goliad. They were too late.

On October 5, when General Cos found out about the Battle of Gonzales, he left the major portion of his arms and supplies at Goliad. He then marched with his troops to San Antonio to support

The Battle of Gonzales was the first of the Texas war for independence from Mexico. This piece of artwork was made in tribute to the people's threat to the Mexican forces to "Come and Take It," referring to their cannon.

the men retreating from Gonzales. Captain George Collingsworth, with about sixty Texan volunteers, arrived at Goliad during the night of October 10, 1835. They forced open the back doors of the fort, and after a short rifle fight, the three Mexican officers and about twenty soldiers surrendered. One Mexican soldier was killed and one colonist wounded. The colonists captured Cos's arms and supplies, but, more important, they now controlled the seacoast of Texas. The Mexicans would not be able

After a short fight, the Texans forced the Mexican soldiers to surrender the fort at Goliad.

to land any reinforcements for General Cos by sea. He would have to be resupplied by the one-hundred-fifty-mile-long passage across the south Texas desert.[3]

Jim Bowie Joins the War

The original force of Texans who fought the Battle of Gonzales was soon joined by many volunteers as the ragtag army of independence moved toward San Antonio. These men elected Stephen F. Austin their commander. Jim Bowie left his home in San Antonio and joined the army on its march. One veteran recalled that "recruits were constantly arriving, singly and in squads, each squad being duly officered . . . we soon had more officers than men."[4] Austin organized the army, now numbering about four hundred fifty men, into two divisions, one commanded by Edward Burleson and the other by Jim Bowie, each of whom was appointed a colonel.[5]

General Cos had upward of six hundred men in San Antonio.[6] The town was guarded by sentinels and companies of infantry entrenched along the roads to the main plaza downtown. General Cos established his headquarters in the deserted mission of the Alamo across the San Antonio River from the main part of the town. It was a formidable position. However, General Cos was forced to send parties out into the countryside every day to get both food for his troops and hay for the horses. Austin decided not to attack

Cos directly but to surround the town and cut off the Mexican troops from food or reinforcements.

Bowie at Mission Espada

On October 22, 1835, Austin sent Bowie's company to scout the lands around two abandoned Spanish missions and to establish an outpost along the roads south of town.[7] The missions lay along the San Antonio River and were now occupied only by poor Mexican farmers and their families. Farther south, along the river, were the rich pastures of the Seguín family ranches. Juan Seguín, a prominent citizen of San Antonio who had fought in the state revolution in May 1835, had joined the Texans against General Cos and offered the resources of the family ranches to the troops of Stephen F. Austin.[8] Erasmo Seguín, Juan's father, later submitted a bill for $3,004 for the oxen, mules, corn, beans, beef, and other supplies he had furnished at this time to Texas.[9]

Bowie and his volunteers left the main camp at the Salado Creek and moved south and camped at mission Espada, six miles south of San Antonio. On October 24 and 25, Stephen Austin sent reinforcements to Bowie. On October 26, the Mexican cavalry attacked the men at mission Espada to cover the arrival of reinforcements moving into San Antonio. To avoid being divided by the Mexican forces who were attacking his small outpost, Austin moved the main body of his army from Salado Creek to mission Espada.[10] At this time, the Texan Army numbered nearly seven hundred men. More were arriving almost daily, some from the settlements of Texas and some from the United States. The main body of the Texan Army barely missed the Mexican cavalry, which quickly raced back into town when the enemy approached.[11]

Bowie at Mission Concepción

General Austin then ordered Jim Bowie to take a party of volunteers to scout along the San Antonio River even closer to town and to return before nightfall.[12] Bowie selected mission Concepción, only a mile outside San Antonio, as their campsite, but he disobeyed Austin's order to return that night.

Early the next morning, they were attacked by a company of Mexican troops. At the first Mexican volley, the Texans quickly retreated to the protection of the nearby riverbank. From the river level they cut steps in its steep dirt bank with their knives and axes. This allowed them to step up and fire over the top at the advancing Mexicans and then step down to reload in the protection of the high riverbank.

The Mexican infantry was dressed in bright blue overcoats with red cuffs and collars. They made a conspicuous target. They carried a short shotgun called a "Brown Bess" that was accurate only at close range. As long as they remained more than several dozen yards away from the Texans, they were harmless. Not so the Texans who were armed with long-range rifles that were accurate at over a hundred yards. It was a critical advantage in battle.[13] Texan James DeShields later described the scene:

> The Mexicans now brought up a brass-ribbed four pounder [small cannon] and opened a rapid fire on our position with grape and canister, which, however, passed harmless over our heads. This gun was being worked eighty or ninety yards from our position and the gunners became targets for the crack riflemen along that part of the line nearest the cannon. It seemed that at one volley every artillery-man hit the dust, and those who took their places shared a like fate. When they were driven back the third and last time, and while their officers were vainly trying to rally them on their colors, which had been placed on the cannon, Jim Bowie shouted, "The cannon, boys! Come on and let's take the cannon." And with a wild cheer the men rushed forward, seized the Mexican color standard, wheeled the gun, which was loaded, and turned it on the enemy who fled in the direction of San Antonio. The fight was over.[14]

The Mexican forces had sixteen killed and a like number wounded.[15] The Texans lost only one man.

During the fight, just before the fog cleared, a runner was sent back to Austin's main camp with the news of the battle. Austin rallied his men and rushed to the scene of the battle, hoping to catch the Mexicans from the rear. The fight ended too soon, and the retreating Mexican infantry fled into San Antonio about an hour before Austin's troops arrived.[16]

Reinforcements and Delay

The next day, October 28, about two hundred new Texan troops under the command of thirty-one-year-old Thomas J. Rusk arrived from Nacogdoches. At this point, the Mexican and Texan forces numbered about the same.[17]

General Austin decided to divide his army. He left Jim Bowie in command of approximately four hundred men at mission Concepción, and he moved with the other half of the army to a position less than a mile north of the town. San Antonio was now effectively cut off from the rest of the world.

On October 30, Jim Bowie moved his men right up to the limits of the town and requested a meeting with General Cos. The two men met, but nothing was decided. Bowie retreated to his camp. In the next few days, General Austin also sent a request for surrender to Cos, who refused even to read it.[18] Cos felt secure inside the well-fortified town, with sixteen cannons ready to fire on the attacking Texans. He knew that the Texans did not have any cannons that could attack his defenses. He could wait for the large body of reinforcements from Mexico that was on its way and then catch and defeat the Texan Army.[19]

Jim Bowie was among those who wanted to attack immediately. There were rumors of quarreling between Bowie and Austin over the matter.[20] On November 2, Bowie's men voted not to attack San

Bowie and his men used the mission at Concepción as their campsite.

Antonio. Bowie, greatly disappointed, resigned his command.[21] Some of the men under Bowie's command started to leave. Most of the others in his camp moved to Austin's position north of town. Austin kept scouts and cavalry patrols active in the south to continue the siege of San Antonio. Bowie remained in camp north of town, as a private. Desertions continued. Austin issued an order allowing no one to pass the guard lines without his written permission. It did little good. In only a couple of days, nearly half the men in Austin's command had left. The number of Austin's troops had decreased to approximately four hundred fifty men.[22]

Sometime around November 12, General Cos sent Colonel Domingo Ugartechea and one hundred soldiers to bring reinforcements from Mexico. Ugartechea evaded the Texan scouts and left undetected. He reached Laredo on November 22. Some friendly Mexicans from town told the Texans of his departure and reported that Ugartechea was not only to bring back reinforcements, but also several strongboxes of gold and silver to pay the troops in San Antonio.[23]

The Grass Fight

On the morning of November 26, Texan scout Erastus "Deaf" Smith was seen, coming across the field at full speed. Making his way to headquarters, he stated that a body of Mexicans was about five miles west, heading toward town.[24] Colonel Edward

Burleson ordered Jim Bowie to intercept the Mexican column of approximately five hundred men before it reached the safety of San Antonio.

It was a wild scene. Bowie quickly chose forty volunteers, but the entire camp started to follow in the hunt for gold. Bowie's men found the Mexican troops at Alazan Creek, a mile west of San Antonio. Bowie ordered an immediate mounted charge. The long rifles of the Texans, so deadly at the battle at mission Concepción, were ineffective in a cavalry charge. They were too long to be effectively fired from horseback.

Instead, Bowie's men charged with sabers, pistols, and knives. The Mexican cavalry fell back and sought cover in a nearby dry creek bed. General Cos, in San Antonio, could see the battle from the bell tower of San Fernando Church. He immediately ordered infantry reinforcements to support the Mexican cavalry. Bowie's men soon found themselves outnumbered and outgunned. Bowie ordered his men to dismount and seek cover in another dry part of the creek bed.

The Mexicans charged Bowie's position, but the Texan long rifles again proved effective from a defensive position. Three times the Mexican charge was repulsed, each time leaving more and more Mexican bodies on the field. Then the rest of the Texan Army arrived on the scene under the command of William H. Jack. From each end, Bowie and

Jack attacked the twelve-foot-deep creek bed that hid the Mexicans, catching them in the middle with nowhere to run. The Mexicans spilled over the top of the creek bed and ran for town. The Texans chased them until more Mexican reinforcements from San Antonio with two field cannons forced them to break off the fight.[25] Creed Taylor remembered:

> The coveted pack train was in our possession. But our chagrin and disgust knew no bounds when we found that instead of silver coin, the packs contained nothing more than grass which was intended for the starving horses of Cos' cavalry.... This ludicrous affair, almost approaching a battle, was then dubbed and is since known in our history as the "Grass Fight."[26]

Bowie Leaves San Antonio

After the Grass Fight, Jim Bowie left the army surrounding San Antonio. He knew that an actual assault on the town was about to happen. Bowie probably had little interest in the actual street battle for San Antonio. He lived there, and the fighting would be conducted through his and his relatives' homes around the plaza downtown. These homes would be destroyed. Many civilian citizens of the town, friends of Bowie, would be placed in danger. Jim Bowie, longtime San Antonio resident Philip Dimmit, and several others were ordered by Stephen F. Austin to inspect the Texan position at Goliad. Bowie and these few men left San Antonio and followed the course of the river southeast toward Goliad. On the way, they searched for Mexican horses.[27] Bowie and Dimmit arrived in Goliad on December 15. Bowie left Goliad alone soon after. No one knows where he went. Perhaps he returned to Louisiana to see his family.[28]

The Battle for San Antonio

The battle for San Antonio took place from December 5 to December 9, 1835. It almost did not happen. After nearly three months of conducting a siege against General Cos inside the town of San Antonio, most of the Texan leaders could not decide whether or not to attack. The Texans always voted on important issues, and for one reason or another, a majority vote to attack San Antonio could never be obtained. Many of the Texans, tired of waiting, left for home for the winter.

At a roll call on the morning of December 4, one volunteer, Ben Milam, a longtime resident of Texas, called out, "Who will go with old Ben Milam into San Antonio?"[29] He was determined to go alone if necessary. By the afternoon, over three hundred men had volunteered.

The next morning, leaving the rest of the Texans in support, Milam's men snuck into town to avoid the Mexican sentries and cannons. For the next three days, the Mexican soldiers and the Texans fought hand to hand in and around the homes by the main plaza. With bayonets and iron bars, the Texans dug through the walls of each house to fire on the soldiers inside and on top. As Bowie had foreseen, the battle destroyed many homes. Ben Milam died from a shot through the head on December 7. Both sides showed tremendous courage, but by the morning of December 9, General Cos hoisted a white flag and agreed to surrender. Cos gave the Texans the money, arms, ammunition, and public property in San Antonio. He agreed to march his men back to the interior of Mexico and never to fight against the Texans again.[30] In fact, he would return to fight again. The Texas Revolution had barely begun.

7

THE TEXAS REVOLUTION

After the victory at San Antonio, several of the Texan leaders felt that an attack on the important Mexican port of Matamoros was the best way to defeat General Santa Anna, who was already rumored to be on his way to Texas. Two hundred or more volunteers from the nearby Mexican states of Nuevo Leon and Tamaulipas were camped between the Nueces River and the Rio Grande, south of San Antonio. They were waiting for someone to lead them back to their home states to spread the revolt against Santa Anna. They would join a Texan attack on Matamoros.

The March on Matamoros

Colonel Frank Johnson, who had received General Cos's surrender in San Antonio, and Colonel James Grant of Parras proposed to lead a march on Matamoros. Johnson received command to lead a volunteer army from the provisional Texas government at San Felipe. When Johnson and Grant left San Antonio on January 3, 1836, they took almost the entire army that had defeated General Cos. Mostly the sick and wounded were all who were left to defend the town. Before they left, they stripped the town of arms, horses, and supplies. They even took the hospital equipment and all the medicine.[1]

Sam Houston, Jim Bowie's old friend, had become the commander of the Texan Army in November. On December 17, Houston, who did not trust either Colonel Johnson or Colonel Grant, sent an order to Bowie to take command of the volunteer army that would march on Matamoros. If Bowie could not gain the allegiance of the volunteers, he was ordered to take charge of the port of Copano nearby so that Johnson and Grant could not get the supplies that were due to arrive at that port. Sam Houston wrote:

> My reason for ordering Colonel Bowie on the service was his familiar acquaintance with the country, as well as the nature of the population through which he must pass, as also their resources; and to this I freely add, there is no man on whose forecast, prudence and valor I place a higher estimate than Colonel Bowie.[2]

Bowie and Houston Work Together

By the time Jim Bowie found out about his new assignment, he had decided that the best time for such a surprise expedition to Matamoros had passed.[3] Bowie returned to San Felipe the first week of 1836 and returned his orders from Houston to the provisional president, Henry Smith, on January 6.[4] President Smith ordered Bowie to return to Goliad.[5]

General Sam Houston had already decided to go to Goliad himself. He left San Felipe on January 8, received Jim Bowie's letter as he was crossing the Colorado River, and reached Goliad on the night of January 14.[6] He met Bowie there. He was immediately informed that Colonel Grant had already moved the body of the Matamoros expeditionary army farther south to the small town of Refugio. Houston went to Refugio and pleaded with the men to give up the idea of attacking Matamoros. He argued that they had too few men as well as too few supplies and arms. They needed horses for the hundred-mile march. They would be caught and defeated by the advancing Mexican Army. Houston argued that even if they were determined to march on Matamoros, they should at least wait for the reinforcements that were due to arrive at the port of Copano.

The men took a vote and most decided to return to Goliad and wait for their reinforcements.

Colonels Grant and Johnson took the few soldiers that remained loyal to them and proceeded toward Matamoros. They were caught by an advancing Mexican Army under the clever and ruthless General José Urrea and soundly defeated. All but a few of these men were killed.

Houston Sends Bowie to the Alamo

Once General Houston had stopped the Texan advance on Matamoros, he ordered Jim Bowie to go to San Antonio with about thirty men. He was to help Lieutenant Colonel James Clinton Neill, the commander there, demolish the fortifications of the Alamo and bring the cannons back to the fort at Goliad.

Houston had already been informed that the Mexican dictator, General Santa Anna, was on his way with a large army headed directly toward San Antonio.[7] Houston hoped never to have to defend the city of San Antonio against the advancing forces of Santa Anna. Houston wanted to make a stand against General Santa Anna at Goliad. The Goliad fort was massive and strong, designed to defend itself against an attack and siege by a superior army. Nearby was the port of Copano, where the needed military supplies that were being bought in the United States were to be landed. To Sam Houston, Goliad was important to defend, but San Antonio was not.

Bowie Decides to Stay and Die

Jim Bowie and some volunteers left for San Antonio on January 17, and arrived on January 19, 1836.[8] Jim Bowie perhaps did not share Sam Houston's conviction that San Antonio was not worth defending. To Sam Houston, San Antonio was just a Mexican town. To Jim Bowie, it was home. It was also the home of Bowie's friends and relatives who were being threatened with General Santa Anna's revenge.

When Bowie arrived in San Antonio, he was impressed with the fortifications that Colonel Neill had been able to construct with the few men who remained after the expedition to Matamoros had left town. He was also impressed with the quality and spirit of the men who were there. These were the men who had been too wounded in the bloody fight for San Antonio to join the expedition to Matamoros. They were the kind of men willing to fight again to keep it. Green Jameson, the chief Texan engineer at the Alamo, had arranged nineteen cannons, mostly captured from General Cos, along the recently reinforced walls of the Alamo. These cannons included one eighteen-pounder. Each cannon could be loaded with small lead balls, nails, or chains—anything iron. This "grapeshot" could kill men who were close together in bunches. Jameson felt that these cannons made the Alamo a much stronger defensive position than Houston thought.

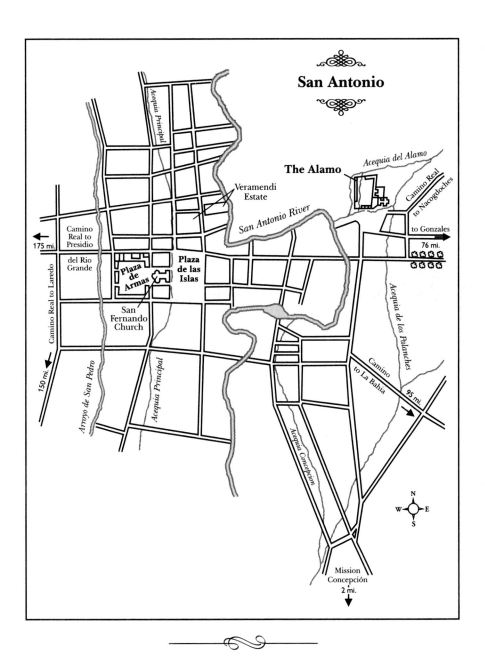

Sam Houston preferred not to defend San Antonio against Mexican forces. To Jim Bowie, however, the city was home to his family and friends and was important to protect.

Jameson wrote General Houston on January 18 that the Texans could "whip 10 to 1 with our artillery."[9]

On February 2, 1836, Bowie wrote a letter to President Henry Smith in San Felipe that spoke of his decision to stay in San Antonio: "Colonel Neill and myself have come to the solemn resolution that we will rather die in these ditches than give it up to the enemy."[10]

William Barret Travis Arrives

President Smith agreed that San Antonio was worth defending. He had already authorized Lieutenant Colonel William Barret Travis to raise a company of men to join those at the Alamo. Travis was only able to recruit thirty men to ride with him. When they arrived on February 3, only a day after Bowie had sent his message to Smith, it must have appeared a good omen to the men working at the Alamo.[11]

Travis found an exciting time in San Antonio when he arrived. By day, the men worked hard to build and reinforce the walls of the mission. Cavalry parties brought beef, hay, and food from the outlying ranches. There was a small society of poor families who lived inside the mission or in shanties outside the walls. They washed clothes, ran errands, and operated the small restaurants that fed the American visitors. In the plaza, across the irrigation canal that separated the Alamo from downtown, the homes of the Veramendis, the Seguíns, the Navarros,

Lieutenant Colonel William Barret Travis arrived on February 3, 1836, with about thirty men to help defend San Antonio.

and many other prominent families hosted parties and conferences.

Davy Crockett Comes With a Fiddle

On January 13, 1836, there was a great commotion in the graveyard on the west side of San Pedro Creek. Fifteen newcomers to town were looking for the Alamo. Among them was Davy Crockett, the famous adventurer and former congressman from Tennessee. He had come with some friends to Texas to fight for independence. He and his men figured that San Antonio was exactly where they wanted to be, right in the middle of the action.

The men in San Antonio knew Crockett by reputation and welcomed him with a party that evening in the streets around the Alamo. They made a large bonfire, and everyone ate and drank. Crockett made an impassioned speech and everyone cheered. Then Crockett pulled out his fiddle and played some popular tunes while everyone danced, told stories, and drank the night away. Crockett was lodged in the home of Erasmo Seguín, and he and his men were soon working hard on the Alamo's fortifications.[12]

On February 10, 1836, a formal party was given in one of the homes in the main square to welcome Crockett to San Antonio. All the eligible young ladies of the town came in their prettiest dresses. The dancing went on well past midnight. Sometime around one in the morning, a courier arrived at the ball with an important letter for Juan Seguín. It was from a

David "Davy" Crockett was a famous frontiersman and a former congressman, who came with some friends to join in the fight for the independence of Texas.

friend of his who was spying on the movements of the Mexican Army, three hundred miles away.

Seguín was not present, but the courier allowed Jim Bowie to open and read the letter. Bowie read it and beckoned to Travis, who was dancing nearby. Travis said that he did not have time to read letters because he was dancing with the most beautiful lady in San Antonio. Bowie told him that he had better come. Crockett joined Travis and they walked over to where Bowie and the courier were standing. Bowie handed the note to Travis, who read Spanish, and then he translated what it said to Crockett. It was short and to the point. General Antonio López de Santa Anna was marching to San Antonio with thirteen thousand men. Travis looked up and said that it would take between thirteen and fourteen days to march that many men to San Antonio. Let us dance tonight and worry about it tomorrow, he said. Soon everyone in the room had heard the news. The dancing continued until seven in the morning.[13]

Daylight brought to these men the realization that if they stayed in San Antonio, they were going to die. Some of these men had fathers and grandfathers who had fought—and, in some cases, died—in the American Revolution for the idea of political independence. But this was different. In a war, most soldiers go into battle with the idea that even though they are willing to die for what they believe in, they will survive. With this attitude, death in battle is a surprise. But there would be no surprise for the defenders of the Alamo. Death would be certain. There were one hundred fifty defenders. The enemy was estimated at thirteen thousand. Dawn on February 11, 1836, brought the light of certainty that each of them was going to die for Texas. Each of them would have a couple of weeks until the enemy arrived to think about it.

That day Colonel Neill left about noon. He had received an express message that his family was sick and needed him. He promised to be back in twenty days at the latest. He asked Lieutenant Colonel Travis, the highest ranking officer in San Antonio, to assume command. Bowie kept command of the volunteers who had come to San Antonio with him from Goliad.[14] Travis wrote President Smith, telling him of Colonel Neill's departure and his appointment as commander. Jim Bowie was older, more experienced, and more popular with the men than Travis. "I feel myself delicately and awkwardly situated," Travis wrote. He requested Smith to send him confirmation of his command. He also wrote that reinforcements were needed, but that even if they did not come, "I am determined to defend it to the last, and, should Bejar [San Antonio] fall, your friend will be buried beneath its ruins."[15]

Bowie Elected Commander

Travis did not wait for President Smith's confirmation of his command. He gathered the men and told them that if they were not satisfied with him in command, they could vote to see who would lead them. Only Bowie's volunteers voted, and they voted for Bowie.[16] It appears that the election took place while the men were not very sober. Bowie and his men had reacted to the news of their coming deaths with a party. They were getting drunk. The rest of the town was already in an uproar. The news of Santa Anna's approach was all over town. Some families were loading their possessions into carts and leaving town as quickly as possible. February 12 was also the day that many of the three-month terms of enlistment for the soldiers at San Antonio ended. They had not been paid for months, and they were due seven dollars each. Coupled with the news of Santa Anna's approach, the lack of pay made it seem to some of the soldiers like a good time to go home. They just took their discharge papers and left town.[17]

Bowie Releases the Prisoners

Bowie and his volunteers felt that everyone in town should have the same right to decide to stay or to leave, even the prisoners in the jail. Jim Bowie used his recently acquired power to write his only order as the commander of the Alamo. Addressed to the captains of the various companies of Alamo defenders, it stated:

> You are hereby required to release such Prisoners as may be under your direction, for labor or otherwise.
>
> James Bowie
> Commandant of the volunteer forces of Bejar.[18]

Bowie sent a corporal and some guards and freed D. H. Barre, a private in the army who had been convicted of mutiny. Bowie also freed Antonio Fuentes, recently convicted of theft from a public works project. The judge of the town, Juan Seguín, rearrested Fuentes and put him back in jail. Bowie then called for reinforcements from the Alamo to release Fuentes by force if necessary. J. J. Baugh, the administrative officer of the men at the Alamo, wrote in disgust:

> Bowie immediately sent to the Alamo for troops and they immediately paraded in the Square, under Arms, in a tumultuously and disorderly manner, Bowie, himself, and many of his men, being drunk which has been the case ever since he has been in command.[19]

Fuentes was rereleased. Judge Seguín resigned in protest and told both Bowie and Travis to get another judge. At the same time, Travis took the regular army troops out of town, telling everyone that he was going to the Medina River to find grass and food for the horses. He did not want to get into the middle of an ugly situation, and he must have thought that when everyone sobered up, things would return to normal. He was right. The next day, a sober Jim Bowie signed a formal agreement with Travis to share command of the Alamo. Both men would sign all official correspondence as co-commanders.[20] D. H. Barre soon left town. Fuentes remained free to die with his friends at the Alamo.[21]

Santa Anna Invades San Antonio

On February 16, General Santa Anna crossed the Rio Grande. The next day, General Urrea crossed the river at Matamoros, two hundred miles south near its mouth. For the next couple of days, more families were seen leaving San Antonio. They had put off leaving as long as possible. They carried whatever they could. What they left was stolen by the invading Mexican troops. It appeared that no one was called a coward for leaving. The defenders of the Alamo considered the freedom to decide whether to live or die their special privilege.[22] It would only make it less special to force anyone to join them or look down on anyone who did not. In the evenings, the parties continued both downtown and around the campfires near the Alamo. There were fewer people, but that just made the dances more friendly.

Several companies of Santa Anna's cavalry reached San Antonio on February 23, 1836. They paraded into the main plaza downtown in military order with a marching band parading in front of them. Travis and his men had seen them coming for several hours. By then, all the Texans had retreated behind the fortified walls of the Alamo. Travis wrote a letter for help. He addressed it to President Smith and to the rest of the world: "The enemy in large force is in sight. We want men and provisions. Send them to us. We have 150 men and are determined to defend the Alamo to the last. Give us assistance."[23]

John Sutherland, a courier, quickly mounted his horse and left to carry the note as far as he could. Sutherland and John Smith, a native of Gonzales whom he met on the way, delivered it first at Gonzales, sixty miles away. Copies of the letter were made and other riders carried the note to San Felipe and the other towns in east Texas. They need

Travis's Letter From the Alamo

Bexar, Feby. 24th, 1836

To the People of Texas and All Americans in the World— Fellow Citizens and Compatriots:

> I am besieged, by a thousand or more of the Mexicans under Santa Anna—I have sustained a continual Bombardment & cannonade for 24 hours & have not lost a man. . . .

I shall never surrender or retreat.

> . . . I call on you in the name of Liberty, of patriotism & everything dear to the American character, to come to our aid, with all dispatch. . . . If this call is neglected, I am determined to sustain myself as long as possible & die like a soldier who never forgets what is due to his own honor & that of his country—Victory or Death.

William Barret Travis
LT. COL. COMDT.[24]

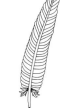

not have bothered. Only in Gonzales would the Alamo defenders find reinforcements.

The Immortal Thirty-two

Around three in the morning on March 1, 1836, thirty-two men and teenagers from Gonzales rode quietly between the Mexicans around the perimeter of the Alamo. There was one fifteen-year-old, William King, and two sixteen-year-olds, Galba Fuqua and John Davis, in the relief party. When they approached the fort, a shot rang out from the walls. One of the riders let out a loud oath in English. That was enough of a password to allow the men inside the walls to know that friends were coming. They opened the gate and the thirty-two rode in to the shouts and cheers of those inside. These men had answered Travis's letter for help. There were already eight men, a woman—Susannah, the wife of Almeron Dickinson, and their baby girl, Angelina, from the tiny colony of Gonzales at the Alamo. Many of these thirty-two men had friends and relatives in the Alamo.

The defenders hoped these would be only the first of many more reinforcements to come. They were wrong. These men who rode to certain death so that they could be with their friends were the only help to come. In all, there were one hundred eighty-four men, fifteen women, and several children who remained in the Alamo to fight approximately twenty-four hundred Mexican troops in San Antonio.[25] That day, March 1, Santa Anna finished posting his string of troops all around the Alamo. He cut off the water supply, and he sent word that he was giving the defenders three days to surrender.[26]

The Line in the Sand

Sometime around the beginning of Santa Anna's three-day cease-fire, Jim Bowie became too sick to stand up. Juana Navarro Alsbury, a sister-in-law of Bowie's who was in the Alamo, said that he had typhoid fever. She nursed him, but Bowie was afraid that the sickness might be passed to others, so he had several soldiers carry him to a small room along the south wall of the Alamo, where he could be away from the others.

During the time of the cease-fire, several more men left the Alamo and never returned. It really was not hard to do. Many of the residents of the small neighborhood around the Alamo still came and went, delivering supplies and food. Some used the chance to spy on the defenders, while others delivered reports about the Mexican Army to Travis. Those who wanted to leave could easily reach the San Antonio River and then escape. It was obvious by March 3, 1836, that no more help was coming. By now, Santa Anna was bombarding the Alamo with small Mexican cannons, seriously weakening the walls. By March 4, cannonballs were often flying

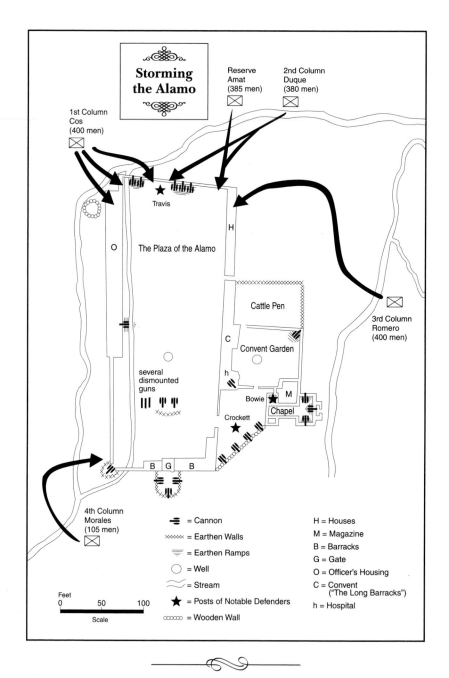

This map shows Santa Anna's plans for storming the Alamo and the positions taken by the Alamo defenders.

right through the walls, although no one inside had yet been killed or even injured.

On March 5, the Mexican artillery was quiet. Everyone could sense that the end of the waiting was near. In the evening, for one last time, Colonel Travis gave the men of the Alamo the chance to leave with honor. He called the men together and drew a long line on the ground with the point of his sword between him and them. He asked all who were willing to die for Texas to step over the line and join him. All but two quickly moved across the line to join him. Henry Rose and Jim Bowie remained. Bowie rose from his sickbed. With tears streaming down his cheeks he said, "Boys, won't none of you help me over there?"[27] Davy Crockett

James Butler Bonham

Many people spent a lot of time trying to get out of the Alamo. James Butler Bonham spent most of his time trying to get in. Twice, Colonel Travis sent Bonham out as a messenger, and twice he fought his way back in, sneaking past the Mexican troops.

James Butler Bonham reentered the Alamo for the last time early on the morning of March 2, 1836. He was killed as a member of a cannon crew near the end of the battle. His body was burned alongside those of his friends.

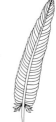

and some others quickly lifted Bowie, on his sickbed, over the line. Henry Rose, however, decided to leave. They opened a window that night and let him go. He was the last to leave.[28] The next morning, March 6, 1836, all of the men who were left in the Alamo died together.

8

SAN JACINTO AND BEYOND

Aﬆer the call went out from the Alamo for help, men began to congregate at Gonzales unaware of the final action on March 6. Gonzales was the Anglo town closest to the Alamo, and the various reinforcements who began to arrive waited there for someone to lead them to the Alamo through the Mexican forces. At dusk on March 11, 1836, just after Sam Houston had arrived to take command of the Texan troops, Anselmo Bogarra and Andres Barcena rode into town with the news of the fall of the defenders.

The next morning, March 12, Houston sent "Deaf" Smith and two others to confirm the story.

About twenty miles from Gonzales, the men met Susannah Dickerson with her infant daughter. They had been in the Alamo and had witnessed the entire battle. They were led to Santa Anna after daybreak on March 7. She confirmed the reports that her husband and the rest of the Alamo defenders had been killed. She told them that General Ramírez y Sesma, with a division of troops, was on his way to Gonzales.

Houston ordered a general retreat to the east. There were only a few wagons available to the troops in Gonzales. These were placed at the disposal of the townspeople to save whatever necessities they could transport. A decision had been made to torch the town in order to deny its resources to the enemy. Most of the people's possessions were simply abandoned. The army burned whatever supplies they could not carry. Three cannons that were held by the Texans were thrown into the river. At eleven o'clock on the night of March 13, the town was deserted. That night and the following morning, about ten men under the direction of Captain John Sharp torched the town.

For over a month, Houston led the Texan Army east. Santa Anna directed his forces to close in on the Texans in a three-pronged attack: General José Francisco Urrea along the coast, General Antonio Gaona to the north, and General Viniente Filisola in the middle. The early spring rains made the ground muddy and the Colorado and Brazos rivers almost impossible to cross. Slowly, the Mexicans began to close in on Houston.

As the Texan Army approached the swampy lands across from Galveston Island, Santa Anna became impatient. He wanted to have the glory of finally defeating Houston and the last of the rebellious Americans. His impatience and pride led him to make a terrible mistake.

Santa Anna took a strike force of troops and rushed ahead of the other Mexican forces so that he would contact Houston first. On April 21, 1836, the two sides—910 Texans and 1,360 Mexicans—were camped three quarters of a mile apart on the plain of San Jacinto. Around three-thirty in the afternoon, at the time most of the Mexican troops, including Santa Anna, were resting, the Texans attacked. The battle lasted only eighteen minutes. It was a slaughter. With cries of "Remember the Alamo," the Texans rushed through the poorly protected defenses of the Mexicans and started to kill the sleeping, retreating enemy. Six hundred thirty were killed, and the rest were captured. The Texans had only nine killed and thirty wounded.

Santa Anna escaped, but he was captured the next day, wearing the uniform of an ordinary soldier. He was identified by his own troops as soon as he was brought into camp. He was taken immediately to Sam Houston, who was one of the wounded. Most of the Texans cried out to hang him right then and

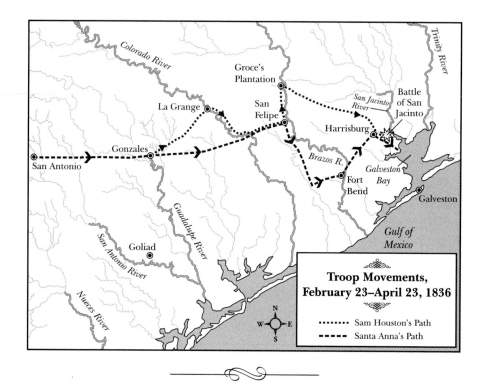

Sam Houston led his forces east through Texas after the loss of the Alamo, finally defeating Santa Anna's troops at the Battle of San Jacinto in April 1836.

there. Houston was smarter. He made a deal with Santa Anna. Houston would send him back to Mexico unharmed if Santa Anna, as the supreme commander of the Mexican Army, would tell the rest of his troops to retreat and leave Texas, and if Santa Anna, as the president of Mexico, would recognize the independence of Texas. Santa Anna agreed. And so the province of Texas became the independent Republic of Texas.[1]

The Wounded at the Alamo
Six weeks after the fall of the Alamo, Dr. James H. Barnard arrived from Goliad to help treat the Mexican wounded. He wrote:

> Yesterday and to-day we have been around with the surgeons of the place to visit the wounded, and a pretty piece of work "Travis, and his faithful few" have made of them. There are now about a hundred here of the wounded. The surgeons tell us that there were four hundred of them brought into the hospital the morning they stormed the Alamo, but I should think from appearance that there must have been more. I see many around the town, who were crippled there, apparently, two or three hundred and the citizens tell me that three or four hundred have died of their wounds.[2]

The heroic sacrifice of the men in the Alamo really did little good in the effort to defeat Santa Anna in military terms. The thirteen days they resisted did not help Houston recruit more men or train or organize them better. Santa Anna's army surely had more than enough men and cannons to defeat the rest of the Texans even after the Alamo defenders had put about a thousand of them out of service. Houston's victory was luck—luck that Santa Anna had been vain and stupid. In the larger picture, however, the sacrifice of the Alamo defenders was crucial for Texas.

This monument, erected on the San Jacinto Battlefield, commemorates the ultimate victory of the Texas defenders, whose success was due, in part, to the heroic sacrifice of men like Jim Bowie.

Today, this monument stands at the Alamo as a tribute to the brave men who gave their lives for Texas independence.

When Travis's letter for help from the Alamo was published in the United States, the image of so few giving their lives against so many inflamed the nation. Thousands of men from both cities and farms who had never heard of Texas took their rifles and left to join the fight. It was all over by the time they got to Texas, but many of them stayed, became citizens of the new country, and helped it survive the first few years of independence.

After the Battle of San Jacinto, Sam Houston wrote a letter to President Andrew Jackson, telling him of Texas independence. When Jackson released the story on May 21, there were wild celebrations in the streets of many cities. On June 18, 1836, Henry Clay rose in Congress and offered a resolution to recognize the new nation of Texas. The motion was approved at the next session in March 1837. Texas was annexed to the United States as the thirty-sixth state on December 29, 1845.[3] This ultimate victory was made possible, in part, by the heroic sacrifice of Jim Bowie and his fellow defenders of the Alamo.

CHRONOLOGY

1796—*April 10*: James Bowie born in Logan County, Kentucky.

1800— Bowie family moves to Spanish Missouri.

1802— Bowie family moves to Louisiana.

1814—*December*: Jim and Rezin Bowie enlist to fight the British at New Orleans.

1815— Jim Bowie sets up a home of his own.

1827— Sandbar Knife Fight.

1828— Bowie arrives in San Antonio.

1831—*January 4*: Juan Martín de Veramendi made vice governor of Coahuila y Texas.

April 25: Bowie marries Ursula de Veramendi in San Antonio.

November–December: San Saba Indian fight.

1832— Expedition against Indians around San Antonio.

August: Battle of Nacogdoches; Bowie escorts Mexican soldiers to San Antonio.

Winter: Bowie travels to Washington, D.C.

1833—*January*: Bowie returns to San Antonio with Sam Houston.

February: Bowie arrives in Saltillo to arrange political coup.

September: Ursula Bowie dies.

1835— *October 3*: Battle of Gonzales begins armed conflict; Bowie joins Austin's army.

December 17: Sam Houston orders Bowie to march to Matamoros.

1836—*January 1*: Bowie receives Houston's orders at Goliad.

January 6: Bowie travels to San Felipe and returns Houston's orders.

January 6–10: President Henry Smith orders Jim Bowie to return to Goliad.

January 10–16: Bowie and Houston in Goliad area to break up Johnson and Grant's plan.

February 2: Bowie writes President Smith that he is determined to stay and die in Alamo defense.

February 12: Men elect Bowie commander.

February 13: Bowie releases prisoners from jail.

February 14: William Barret Travis writes that co-commandancy of the Alamo is formed.

February 16: Santa Anna crosses the Rio Grande.

February 23: Mexican troops sighted.

March 1–3: Bowie sick in bed during Santa Anna's cease-fire.

March 6: Bowie dies in Mexican assault on the Alamo.

CHAPTER NOTES

Chapter 1. The Alamo

1. José Enrique de la Peña, *With Santa Anna in Texas* (College Station: Texas A & M University Press, 1975), p. 52.

2. Walter Prescott Webb, ed., *Handbook of Texas* (Austin: Texas State Historical Society, 1952), vol. 1, p. 22.

3. Amelia Williams, "A Critical Study of the Siege of the Alamo and of the Personnel of its Defenders," *Southwestern Historical Quarterly*, vol. 37, no. 1, July 1933, pp. 41–42.

4. Timothy Matovina, *The Alamo Remembered: Tejano Accounts and Perspectives* (Austin: University of Texas Press, 1995), pp. 42, 60.

5. Williams, p. 43.

6. Frederick C. Chabot, *With the Makers of San Antonio* (San Antonio: Artes Graficas, 1937), pp. 36–37.

7. James DeShields, *Tall Men with Long Rifles* (San Antonio: The Naylor Company, 1935), p. 179.

Chapter 2. Early Life

1. Virgil E. Baugh, *Rendezvous at the Alamo: Highlights in the Lives of Bowie, Crockett, and Travis* (Lincoln: University of Nebraska Press, 1985), pp. 15–16.

2. Ibid., pp. 16–17.

3. Raymond W. Thorp, *Bowie Knife* (Albuquerque: University of New Mexico Press, 1948), p. 118.

4. Baugh, p. 16.

5. Thorp, p. 119.

6. Baugh, p. 17.

7. Thorp, p. 120.

8. Ibid., p. 339.

9. Reginald Horsman, "War of 1812," *Academic American Encyclopedia* (Danbury, Conn.: Grolier, 1997), vol. 20, pp. 25–28.

10. Margaret Swett Henson, *Juan Davis Bradburn* (College Station: Texas A & M University Press, 1982), p. 25.

11. Thorp, p. 121.

12. Ibid., pp. 126, 128–131.

13. Ibid., p. 125.

Chapter 3. Jim Bowie Settles in Texas

1. Evelyn Brogan, *James Bowie: A Hero of the Alamo* (San Antonio: Theodore Kunzman, 1922), pp. 33–34.

2. Jack Jackson, *Los Mesteños* (College Station: Texas A & M University Press, 1986), p. 541.

3. Hans Peter Nielsen Gammel, ed., *Laws of Texas* (Austin: Gammel Book Co., 1898–1909), vol. 1, pp. 167–169.

4. Virginia H. Taylor, *The Spanish Archives of the General Land Office of Texas* (Austin: Lone Star Press, 1955), pp. 60–62.

5. Walter Prescott Webb, ed., *Handbook of Texas* (Austin: Texas State Historical Society, 1952), vol. 2, p. 837.

6. J. Frank Dobie, "James Bowie, Big Dealer," *Southwestern Historical Quarterly*, vol. 60, no. 3, January 1957, p. 344.

7. Thomas W. Streeter, *Bibliography of Texas: 1745–1845* (Woodbridge, Conn.: Research Publications, Inc., 1955), vol. 4, p. 256.

8. Antonio Menchaca, *Memoirs* (San Antonio: Yanaguana Society, 1937), p. 21.

9. Brogan, p. 34.

10. Joseph Martin Dawson, *José Antonio Navarro* (Waco, Tex.: Baylor University Press, 1969), p. 32.

11. Brogan, p. 35.

12. Ibid.

Chapter 4. Indian Fighter

1. J. Frank Dobie, "James Bowie, Big Dealer," *Southwest Historical Quarterly*, vol. 60, no. 3, January 1957, p. 347.

2. Mary Austin Holley, *Texas* (Lexington, Ky.: L. Clarke & Co., 1836), pp. 161–173.

3. John Henry Brown, *History of Texas, From 1685 to 1892* (St. Louis: L. E. Daniel, 1892), pp. 170–175.

4. Raymond W. Thorp, *Bowie Knife* (Albuquerque: University of New Mexico Press, 1948), p. 125.

5. Brown, pp. 170–175.

6. Virgil E. Baugh, *Rendezvous at the Alamo: Highlights in the Lives of Bowie, Crockett, and Travis* (Lincoln: University of Nebraska Press, 1985), p. 77.

Chapter 5. Political Dynasty and Tragedy

1. Thomas W. Streeter, *Bibliography of Texas: 1745–1845* (Woodbridge, Conn.: Research Publications, Inc., 1955), vol. 4, p. 256.

2. Bexar Archives, August 20, 1832, microfilm duplicate: Reel 152, Frames 0676-0679.

3. Hans Peter Nielsen Gammel, ed., *Laws of Texas* (Austin: Gammel Book Co., 1898–1909), vol. 1, pp. 329–342.

4. Raymond W. Thorp, *Bowie Knife* (Albuquerque: University of New Mexico Press, 1948), pp. 113–114.

5. Ibid., pp. 126–127.

6. John McFarland, *McFarland Journal* (San Antonio: Yanaguana Society, 1942), p. xxxvii.

7. Ibid.

8. Gammel, vol. 1, p. 207.

9. Vito Alessio Robles, *Coahuila y Texas desde la consumacion de la Independencia hasta el tratado de paz de Guadalupe Hidalgo* (Mexico D.F: Artes Grafica, 1946), vol. 1, pp. 442–444.

10. Walter Prescott Webb, ed., *Handbook of Texas* (Austin: Texas State Historical Society, 1952), vol. 2, p. 837.

11. Margaret Swett Henson, *Samuel May Williams: Early Texas Entrepreneur* (College Station: Texas A & M Press, 1976), p. 97.

12. J. Frank Dobie, "James Bowie, Big Dealer," *Southwestern Historical Quarterly*, vol. 60, no. 3, January 1957, p. 347.

13. Charles Adam Gulick, ed., *Papers of Mirabeau Buonaparte Lamar* (Austin: A. C. Baldwin, 1922–1927), vol. 5, p. 358.

14. Webb, vol. 1, pp. 197, 663.

15. Hobart Huson, *A Comprehensive History of Refugio County* (Woodsboro, Tex.: Rooke Foundation, 1953–1956), vol. 1, pp. 212–213.

16. Harriet Smither, ed., "Diary of Adolphus Sterne," *Southwestern Historical Quarterly*, vol. 30, no. 2, October 1926, pp. 219, 307.

17. John Jenkins, ed., *The Papers of the Texas Revolution* (Austin: Presidial Press, 1973), vol. 1, pp. 301–302.

18. Dobie, pp. 347–348.

Chapter 6. Early Conflicts of the Texas Revolution

1. Walter Prescott Webb, ed., *Handbook of Texas* (Austin: Texas State Historical Society, 1952), vol. 1, p. 707.

2. Ibid.

3. Ibid., pp. 699–700.

4. Paul D. Lack, *The Texas Revolutionary Experience* (College Station: Texas A & M University Press, 1992), p. 112.

5. Ibid., pp. 112–113.

6. Alwyn Barr, *Texans in Revolt* (Austin: University of Texas Press, 1990), p. 27.

7. Martha Anne Turner, *William Barret Travis: His Sword and His Pen* (Waco, Tex.: Texian Press, 1972), p. 134.

8. Ibid.

9. Lack, p. 188.

10. Turner, p. 134.

11. Barr, p. 21.

12. Turner, pp. 134–135.

13. Phillip Haythornthwaite, *The Alamo and the War of Texan Independence 1835–1836* (London: Osprey Publishing Ltd., 1986), pp. 44–46.

14. James DeShields, *Tall Men With Long Rifles* (San Antonio: The Naylor Company, 1935), pp. 43–45.

15. Ibid., p. 45.

16. Ibid., p. 43.

17. Barr, p. 27.

18. Mary Rowena Green, *Samuel Maverick, Texan: 1803–1870* (San Antonio: privately printed, 1952), p. 34.

19. Steven Hardin, *Texian Iliad* (Austin: University of Texas Press, 1994), p. 53.

20. Green, pp. 35–36.

21. John Jenkins, ed., *The Papers of the Texas Revolution* (Austin: Presidial Press, 1973), vol. 2, pp. 297, 300–301.

22. Ibid., p. 310.

23. DeShields, p. 47.

24. Cleburne Huston, *Deaf Smith: Incredible Texas Spy* (Waco, Tex.: Texian Press, 1973), p. 31.

25. Hardin, pp. 64–66.

26. DeShields, p. 48.

27. Barr, p. 41; Hardin, p. 64.

28. Hobart Huson, *Captain Philip Dimmitt's Commandancy of Goliad, 1835–1836* (Austin: Von Boeckmann-Jones, 1974), p. 203.

29. Webb, vol. 1, p. 154.

30. Ibid.

Chapter 7. The Texas Revolution

1. Steven Hardin, *Texian Iliad* (Austin: University of Texas Press, 1994), p. 107.

2. John Henry Brown, *Life and Times of Henry Smith* (Dallas: A. D. Aldridge & Co., 1887), p. 215.

3. Henderson K. Yoakum, *History of Texas* (New York: Redfield, 1856), vol. 2, p. 47.

4. Martha Anne Turner, *William Barret Travis: His Sword and His Pen* (Waco, Tex.: Texian Press, 1972), p. 158.

5. John Jenkins, ed., *The Papers of the Texas Revolution* (Austin: Presidial Press, 1973), vol. 4, p. 236.

6. Turner, p. 159.

7. Brown, p. 210.

8. Hardin, p. 111.

9. Jenkins, vol. 4, pp. 58–61.

10. Ibid., pp. 236–238.

11. Hardin, p. 117.

12. Timothy Matovina, *The Alamo Remembered: Tejano Accounts and Perspectives* (Austin: University of Texas Press, 1995), pp. 60, 118.

13. Ibid., p. 118.

14. Jenkins, vol. 4, p. 303.

15. Ibid., p. 318.

16. Ibid., p. 320.

17. Ibid.

18. Ibid., pp. 320–321.

19. Ibid.

20. Ibid., p. 339.

21. Matovina, p. 35.

22. Hardin, p. 121.

23. Jenkins, vol. 4, p. 420.

24. Quoted in William C. Davis, *Three Roads to the Alamo: The Lives and Fortunes of David Crockett, James Bowie, and William Barret Travis* (New York: HarperCollins Publishers, 1998), p. 541.

25. Walter Lord, *A Time to Stand* (Lincoln: University of Nebraska Press, 1961), p. 210.

26. Matovina, p. 81.

27. Ibid., p. 60.

28. Ibid., p. 82.

Chapter 8. San Jacinto and Beyond

1. Walter Prescott Webb, ed., *Handbook of Texas* (Austin: Texas State Historical Society, 1952), vol. 2, p. 554.

2. José Enrique de la Peña, *With Santa Anna in Texas* (College Station: Texas A & M University Press, 1975), pp. 60–63.

3. Webb, vol. 1, pp. 51–52.

GLOSSARY

adobe—Sun-dried bricks, made from a mixture of clay and straw, used as a building material.

alcalde—The mayor or chief administrative official in a Spanish or Mexican town.

archives—A collection of official records and other papers of a government or business.

barter—To trade, rather than pay, for something.

bayonet—A sharp blade attached to the front of a rifle for hand-to-hand combat.

Castilian—A resident, or descendant of a resident, of Castile, a province in Spain.

cavalry—Soldiers who fight on horseback.

convert—A person who has been persuaded to adopt a religion, political party, or any new idea.

courier—A messenger.

dialect—A way of speaking the same language differently that indicates where the speaker lives.

federal—Form of government in which states recognize the authority of a central authority while retaining certain powers for themselves.

fluent—Able to speak a language well.

foraging—Searching for food or provisions.

Franciscan—A member of the order of monks founded by St. Francis of Assisi who established Spanish missions in Texas.

frontier—The area just beyond settlement.

gangrene—Decay, and eventual death, of tissue following injury or disease, caused by insufficient blood supply.

irrigation—A system that uses ditches, pipes, or streams to supply water to dry land.

league—A unit of distance equal to 2.2 miles.

militia—An army made up of volunteers as opposed to professional soldiers.

mission—A compound housing missionaries sent by a church to the frontier or a foreign country to gain converts for a religion.

pastime—A pleasurable activity one pursues in spare time.

province—A territory governed by a country.

pyre—A fire for burning corpses.

saber—A heavy sword with a one-edged blade.

sacristy—The room in a church used to store sacred vessels and vestments or clothing.

sentinels—Look-outs.

smuggling—Bringing trade goods into a country without paying a tax.

snare—Trap.

Tejano—A Mexican born in Texas.

FURTHER READING

Books

Barr, Alwyn. *Texans in Revolt: The Battle for San Antonio, 1835*. Austin: University of Texas Press, 1990.

Baston, James L. *James Bowie and the Sandbar Fight: Birth of the James Bowie Legend & Bowie Knife*. Madison, Ala.: Batson Engineering & Metalworks, 1992.

Baugh, Virgil E. *Rendezvous at the Alamo: Highlights in the Lives of Bowie, Crockett, and Travis*. Lincoln: University of Nebraska Press, 1985.

Davis, William C. *Three Roads to the Alamo: The Saga of Davy Crockett, Jim Bowie, and William Travis*. New York: HarperCollins Publishers, 1998.

Flynn, Jean. *Jim Bowie: A Texas Legend*. Burnet, Tex.: Eakin Press, 1980.

Sorrels, Roy. *The Alamo in American History*. Springfield, N.J.: Enslow Publishers, Inc., 1996.

Internet Addresses

The Alamo: Five Hours That Changed History. n.d. <http://numedia.tddc.net/alamo/> (October 1, 1998).

Center for American History, The University of Texas at Austin. *Texas, Texans, and the Alamo*. June 11, 1996. <http://mahogany.lib.utexas.edu:1000/Libs/CAH/texas/cah_texas1.html> (October 1, 1998).

Daughters of the Republic of Texas. *DRT Library Homepage*. "The Alamo Library." 1997. <http://drtl.org> (October 1, 1998).

INDEX